U•X•L Encyclopedia of
U.S. History

U·X·L Encyclopedia of U.S. History

VOLUME 4: H–J

Sonia Benson, Daniel E. Brannen Jr., and Rebecca Valentine

Lawrence W. Baker and Sarah Hermsen, Project Editors

U·X·L
A part of Gale, Cengage Learning

Detroit • New York • San Francisco • New Haven, Conn • Waterville, Maine • London

GALE
CENGAGE Learning™

U•X•L Encyclopedia of U.S. History

Sonia Benson, Daniel E. Brannen Jr., and Rebecca Valentine

Project Editors: Lawrence W. Baker and Sarah Hermsen

Editorial: Julie Carnagie

Rights Acquisition and Management: Margaret Chamberlain-Gaston, Kelly A. Quin, and Jhanay Williams

Composition: Evi Seoud

Manufacturing: Rita Wimberley

Imaging: Lezlie Light

Product Design: Jennifer Wahi

Cover Design: Rokusek Design

For product information and technology assistance, contact us at Gale Customer Support, 1-800-877-4253.
For permission to use material from this text or product, submit all requests online at www.cengage.com/permissions.
Further permissions questions can be emailed to permissionrequest@cengage.com.

While every effort has been made to ensure the reliability of the information presented in this publication, Gale, a part of Cengage Learning, does not guarantee the accuracy of the data contained herein. Gale accepts no payment for listing; and inclusion in the publication of any organization, agency, institution, publication, service, or individual does not imply endorsement of the editors or publisher. Errors brought to the attention of the publisher and verified to the satisfaction of the publisher will be corrected in future editions.

LIBRARY OF CONGRESS CATALOGING-IN-PUBLICATION DATA

Benson, Sonia.
    UXL encyclopedia of U.S. history / Sonia Benson, Daniel E. Brannen Jr., and Rebecca Valentine ; Lawrence W. Baker and Sarah Hermsen, project editors.
       p. cm. --
    Includes bibliographical references and index.
    ISBN 978-1-4144-3043-0 (set) -- ISBN 978-1-4144-3044-7 (vol. 1) -- ISBN 978-1-4144-3045-4 (vol. 2) -- ISBN 978-1-4144-3046-1 (vol. 3) -- ISBN 978-1-4144-3047-8 (vol. 4) -- ISBN 978-1-4144-3048-5 (vol. 5) -- ISBN 978-1-4144-3049-2 (vol. 6) -- ISBN 978-1-4144-3050-8 (vol. 7) -- ISBN 978-1-4144-3051-5 (vol. 8)
       1. United States -- History -- Encyclopedias, Juvenile. I. Brannen, Daniel E., 1968- II. Valentine, Rebecca. III. Title. IV. Title: UXL encyclopedia of US history. V. Title: Encyclopedia of U.S. history.

E174.B46 2008
973.03--dc22   2008022347

Gale
27500 Drake Rd.
Farmington Hills, MI 48331-3535

ISBN-13: 978-1-4144-3043-0 (set)   ISBN-10: 1-4144-3043-4 (set)
ISBN-13: 978-1-4144-3044-7 (vol. 1)   ISBN-10: 1-4144-3044-2 (vol. 1)
ISBN-13: 978-1-4144-3045-4 (vol. 2)   ISBN-10: 1-4144-3045-4 (vol. 2)
ISBN-13: 978-1-4144-3046-1 (vol. 3)   ISBN-10: 1-4144-3046-9 (vol. 3)
ISBN-13: 978-1-4144-3047-8 (vol. 4)   ISBN-10: 1-4144-3047-7 (vol. 4)
ISBN-13: 978-1-4144-3048-5 (vol. 5)   ISBN-10: 1-4144-3048-5 (vol. 5)
ISBN-13: 978-1-4144-3049-2 (vol. 6)   ISBN-10: 1-4144-3049-3 (vol. 6)
ISBN-13: 978-1-4144-3050-8 (vol. 7)   ISBN-10: 1-4144-3050-7 (vol. 7)
ISBN-13: 978-1-4144-3051-5 (vol. 8)   ISBN-10: 1-4144-3051-5 (vol. 8)

This title is also available as an e-book.
ISBN-13: 978-1-4144-3274-8, ISBN-10: 1-4144-3274-7
Contact your Gale, a part of Cengage Learning, sales representative for ordering information.

Printed in the United States of America
1 2 3 4 5 6 7 12 11 10 09 08

Contents

VOLUME 5: K–M

VOLUME 7: R–S

Reader's Guide

U•X•L Encyclopedia of U.S. History introduces students to the history of the United States from pre-Colonial America to present day. This 8-volume set explores the timeline of America: its founders, key historical figures, wars, events, political environment, economy, and culture. Entries were selected with guidance from the National Council for the Social Studies (NCSS) Curriculum Standards for Social Studies—Middle School, which were adopted in 2002. The NCSS standards' eras are: Three Worlds Meet (Discovery of the New World, beginnings to 1620); Colonization and Settlement (1585–1763); Revolution and the New Nation (1754–1820s); Expansion and Reform (1801–61); Civil War and Reconstruction (1850–77); the Development of the Industrial United States (1870–1900); the Emergence of Modern America (1890–1930); the Great Depression and World War II (1929–45); Postwar United States (1945 to the early 1970s); and Contemporary United States (1968 to the present).

U•X•L Encyclopedia of U.S. History features nearly 700 entries—arranged alphabetically across the set—with more than 400 images and maps to help better illustrate the text. Each entry contains bolded terms that indicate cross-references to other entries within this set. In addition, several sidebar boxes offer additional insight into the people, places, and events that have occurred in American history. All eight volumes contain a general bibliography and a comprehensive cumulative subject index that provides easy access to subjects discussed throughout *U•X•L Encyclopedia of U.S. History.*

Acknowledgments

Much appreciation goes to authors Sonia Benson, Daniel E. Brannen Jr., and Rebecca Valentine. Dan Brannen is grateful to project editor Larry Baker, who makes his challenging role seem easy, thus easing the writer's task. Warm regards to Phil, film lover and fellow Coppola fan. Kisses to Kaya, Malina, and Liam, for punctuating long working spells with riveting Italian soccer matches over homebaked pizze and calzoni. To Jen, who shouldered countless tasks to make possible this book and our life in the Desert Ocean: ti amo molto e sempre! Rebecca Valentine thanks Max, Tuck, Tavia, and Bella, who managed without her more than they would have liked.

Additional thanks go to copyeditors Carol Brennan, Anne Davidson, Jessica Hornik Evans, Christa Gainor, Erika-Marie S. Geiss, Ellen Henderson, and Leslie Joseph; proofers Leslie Joseph and Amy Marcaccio Keyzer; the indexers from Factiva, a Dow Jones Company; and typesetter Datapage Technologies International, Inc.

Recognition is also given to the following advisors, whose comments and suggestions helped shape *U•X•L Encyclopedia of U.S. History*:

- Carol Deviney, Librarian/Teacher, Murphy Middle School/Plano ISD, Murphy, Texas
- Maria Kardick, Librarian, Eighth Grade Center, Spring-Ford School District, Royersford, Pennsylvania
- Nina Levine, Library Media Specialist, Blue Mountain Middle School, Cortlandt Manor, New York
- Jacqueline A. Plourde, Retired Director, Learning Resource Center, Madison Junior High School, Naperville, Illinois

Comments and Suggestions

We welcome your comments on *U•X•L Encyclopedia of U.S. History* and suggestions for other topics to consider. Please write: Editors, *U•X•L Encyclopedia of U.S. History,* U•X•L, 27500 Drake Rd., Farmington Hills, Michigan 48331-3535; call toll free: (800) 877-4253; fax to (248) 699-8097; or send e-mail via http://www.gale.cengage.com.

U·X·L Encyclopedia of U.S. History

H

Alexander Hamilton

Alexander Hamilton is counted as one of the founding fathers of the United States of America. Extremely vocal and active in politics, his vision of government shaped the American nation as it is today. His legal and political theories guided many of the nation's leading politicians of his time, yet he also attracted a vocal and popular opposition.

Early years

Alexander Hamilton was born on January 11, 1755, on the island of Nevis in the British West Indies. He was the son of James and Rachel Hamilton He had a difficult childhood on the neighboring Danish island of Saint Croix. His father abandoned the family when Alexander was ten, and his mother died three years later in 1768.

Hamilton's natural intelligence, ambition, and remarkable business judgment inspired relatives and prominent citizens to send Hamilton to a private school in **New Jersey**. He later enrolled at King's College (now Columbia University) in 1773. In 1780, Hamilton married Elizabeth Schuyler, the daughter of **American Revolution** general and **New York** politician Philip Schuyler (1733–1804). Hamilton was admitted to the bar to practice law in 1782, but he soon turned to politics.

A politician

Hamilton became interested in politics as a student at King's College, where he wrote his first pamphlets defending the colonists' War of Independence, or the American Revolution (1775–83). These writings

Alexander Hamilton, one of the founding fathers of the United States, was the first secretary of the treasury.
AP IMAGES

captured the attention of General **George Washington** (1732–1799). At only twenty-two years of age, Hamilton joined the general's military staff as a lieutenant colonel. He became invaluable to Washington during his four years of service. The relationship they established during this time later enabled Hamilton to pursue politics as a career.

Hamilton supported the cause of the revolution, but he eventually criticized the American government set up in 1781 under the **Articles of Confederation** (the forerunner to the U.S. **Constitution**). He felt government under the articles was weak, and so he encouraged a change.

As one of New York's delegates to the **Constitutional Convention** in 1787, Hamilton proposed an extraordinarily powerful national government, one similar to a monarchy (a government ruled by a single person, such as a king or queen, with absolute power). The Constitution created a more democratic government, but Hamilton supported it. A series of essays he wrote with **Virginia** politician and future U.S. president **James Madison** (1751–1836) and Secretary of Foreign Affairs John Jay (1745–1829) proved to be very influential in the state conventions that met to approve the new Constitution. These eighty-five essays, the *Federalist Papers,* were published in a New York newspaper between October 1787 and May 1788. Credited with writing two-thirds of the essays, Hamilton used them to explain the powers of three branches of government under the proposed Constitution.

America's first secretary of the treasury

George Washington became president in 1789 and named Hamilton to be the first secretary of the treasury. It was a position Hamilton took seriously, and he worked swiftly to establish a strong national economy.

Hamilton believed the federal government should promote a strong economy by bolstering commerce. His belief in the connection between national power and commerce meant he did not limit his involvement to domestic financial policies. Hamilton injected himself into every major decision on financial, domestic, and foreign policy that could help make the United States a commercial powerhouse. To achieve such results, Hamilton interpreted the Constitution to give Congress almost unlimited legislative power. His aggressive policies and elitist politics created enemies among politicians and people who wanted government to be stronger at the state and local levels rather than at the federal level.

Even after retiring from the treasury position in 1795, Hamilton maintained his influence in national politics. He remained an important leader of the **Federalist Party**, which he had formed, by advising President Washington, President **John Adams** (1735–1826; served 1797–1801), and various Federalist members of Congress. Hamilton's influence caused problems within President Adams's administration and within the Federalist Party itself. Several important leaders became political opponents of Hamilton, including Adams, President **Thomas Jefferson** (1743–1826; served 1801–9), and Vice President **Aaron Burr** (1756–1836).

The duel

Hamilton became an outspoken critic of Burr, a personal and political rival. Burr's politics vacillated, and he held governmental offices as both a Federalist and a Republican (the opposing political party at the time). In 1804, Hamilton criticized a Federalist plan to support Burr for governor of New York. (Burr was not being renominated as vice president.) Burr challenged Hamilton to a duel after Hamilton refused to apologize for scornful remarks he had made. On July 11, 1804, in Weehawken, New Jersey, Burr shot and wounded Hamilton. Hamilton died the next day in New York City.

Warren G. Harding

Warren G. Harding served as president just under two and a half years before dying in office. His administration is most remembered for its scandals.

Newspaper man

Harding was born on November 2, 1865, and was one of eight children of an **Ohio** doctor and his wife. At sixteen, Harding attended Ohio

Warren G. Harding's presidency was filled with scandal and he died after only two and a half years in office.
THE LIBRARY OF CONGRESS

Central College. He graduated in 1882 and taught school for one term before recognizing that teaching did not suit him well.

With a loan from his father, Harding purchased the *Marion Daily Star* in Marion, Ohio, in 1884. It was a failing newspaper, but with the help of two friends, Harding entered into the newspaper publishing business. His partners left the venture within a few months, but Harding stayed on to build the newspaper into a success by 1890. He married Florence Kling DeWolfe in 1891 and joined several civic and service organizations. Harding became well known in Marion.

Enters politics

Harding's political influence increased throughout the 1890s. He won a seat in the Ohio senate in 1899 and served two terms. In 1903, he was elected lieutenant governor of Ohio. Harding was popular among Ohio Republicans and his easygoing style appealed to leaders.

Beginning in 1905, Harding left politics for five years to focus on running his newspaper. It had become an important paper throughout the state of Ohio, primarily because of Harding's favorable reputation. In 1912, his name became known throughout the country when he nominated **William Howard Taft** (1857–1930; served 1909–13) for president at the Republican National Convention. Harding was elected to the U.S. Senate in 1914 and moved to **Washington, D.C.**

Senator Harding did not impress anyone with his performance. But when he voted in favor of the United States joining the **League of Nations** (an international organization favored by Democratic president **Woodrow Wilson** [1856–1924; served 1913–21] that promoted international peace and security) in 1916, he was looked upon favorably.

Harding announced his presidential candidacy in 1919 and received the nomination in 1920. He beat his Democratic opponent, Ohio governor James M. Cox (1870–1957), by receiving more popular (individual) votes than any candidate of any preceding presidential election.

Conservative and scandalous

Harding supported a conservative financial program that included cutbacks in government spending, higher tariff (tax on imported goods) rates, and corporate (business) tax reduction. By signing the Budget and Accounting Act of 1921, he created a Bureau of the Budget accountable to the president, which made it easier to keep track of spending. Harding vetoed the 1922 Soldier's Bonus Bill, which would have paid a cash bonus to veterans of **World War I** (1914–18).

By 1923, the United States's economy had turned around from one of hardship to one of prosperity. Newspapers praised Harding for the improvement. Within government, however, the picture was not so rosy. Rumor reached Harding that some of his friends were using their positions of power for their own personal glory and improvement.

One scandal in particular overshadowed the Harding administration. Secretary of the Interior Albert Fall (1861–1944) improperly released government oil reserves in Teapot Dome, **Wyoming**, and Elk Hills, **California**, to private interests. And although Harding was not directly involved, he shouldered the blame because he knowingly appointed his friends to positions for which they were not skilled.

The Teapot Dome Scandal had not yet broken publicly, but privately Harding was nervous. He and his wife took a long-planned cross-country trip to the **Alaska** territory in June 1923. On the way home, while at a layover in San Francisco, Harding suffered a heart attack. He died on August 2 in his hotel room. Soon thereafter, the scandal broke, and Harding's reputation suffered greatly.

Harlem Renaissance

The Harlem Renaissance refers to a time period that spanned the 1920s and early 1930s when African American artists and their work flourished. Though largely considered a literary movement, the Harlem Renaissance actually included philosophers, intellectuals, photographers, musicians, and other performance artists as well as those involved in the visual arts. During its heyday, the movement was referred to as the New Negro Movement. The alternate name was eventually given because the African American migration to northern cities in the early 1920s brought many blacks to Harlem, or upper Manhattan, **New York**. As a result, the two square miles between 114th and 156th Streets of Harlem

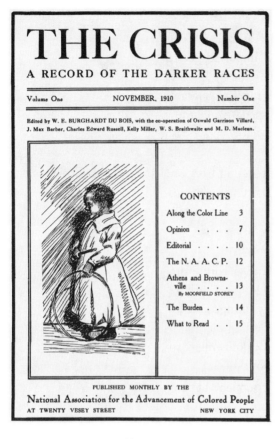

THE CRISIS

A RECORD OF THE DARKER RACES

Volume One   NOVEMBER, 1910   Number One

Edited by W. E. BURGHARDT DU BOIS, with the co-operation of Oswald Garrison Villard, J. Max Barber, Charles Edward Russell, Kelly Miller, W. S. Braithwaite and M. D. Maclean.

CONTENTS

Along the Color Line   3

Opinion   7

Editorial   10

The N. A. A. C. P.   12

Athens and Browns-
    ville   13
    By MOORFIELD STOREY

The Burden   .   .   .   14

What to Read   .   .   15

PUBLISHED MONTHLY BY THE

National Association for the Advancement of Colored People

AT TWENTY VESEY STREET   NEW YORK CITY

W. E. B. DuBois and his influential work with the NAACP's journal The Crisis *is considered by many as inspiration for the Harlem Renaissance.*

became known throughout the world as a cultural metropolis.

For white America, the Harlem Renaissance provided the gateway into an unfamiliar culture that was a major ingredient of the country's "melting pot" (society of many and various cultures and ethnicities). The movement introduced millions of Americans to literature, music, and art that had never before been seen, much less understood. In limited scope, the era helped erase some of the stereotypes assigned to the African American community. White Americans were able to recognize the talent, ability, and giftedness of the Harlem Renaissance's key figures, who in turn stepped forward to represent an entire race.

The movement was arguably more important to African Americans in that it allowed them to claim their heritage and develop their cultural and ethnic identity without feeling the need to hide who they were. For the first time in American history, African Americans were being celebrated for their contributions to society.

Culture and politics entwine

What sets the Harlem Renaissance apart from other cultural movements throughout American history is the fact that at the same time, major political changes were taking place.

The **National Association for the Advancement of Colored People** (NAACP) was established in 1909, and it remained in the forefront of the civil rights struggle. Marcus Garvey (1887–1940) added to the political mix when he began advocating for African colonization and encouraged all African Americans to unite and form their own nation and government. Garvey's politics were controversial, yet the organization he founded in 1914, the Universal Negro Improvement Association, grew to include four million members by 1920. Black nationalism (strong allegiance to and identification with the African American culture, to the exclusion of all other races) was a major influence on the Harlem Renaissance.

Given the tumultuous state of politics, much of the art—particularly the literature—generated throughout the Harlem Renaissance was political in nature. Other participants used their art in an attempt to correct unflattering or distorted ideas of their race and heritage. Garvey himself publicly criticized those African Americans who he felt exploited (used at their own expense) their intelligence and art by giving in to the demands of white audiences. In his eyes, these people betrayed their roots and identity in exchange for fame.

Key figures in the Renaissance

There are many influential figures from the Harlem Renaissance. Considered by many historians and experts to be the inspiration for the Harlem Renaissance, W. E. B. Du Bois (1868–1963) secured a seat for himself at the forefront of early twentieth-century philosophical thought. The African American community embraced Du Bois as its intellectual leader, and as editor-in-chief for twenty-five years of the NAACPs journal the *Crisis,* he single-handedly was responsible for publishing some of the movement' most gifted and respected writers. Among them were poet Langston Hughes (1902–1967) and writer/philosopher Jean Toomer (1894–1967). Both men wrote of their experiences as African Americans in a white society. Du Bois himself was a talented writer, though his philosophy known as the Talented Tenth made him a somewhat controversial figure. According to his theory, the Negro race would be saved only by its exceptional men, who would pull the entire race into equality with whites. This small, elite group of literary and intellectual geniuses, he believed, had to be groomed and supported by the less-intelligent masses.

Other key authors of the Harlem Renaissance included Countee Cullen (1903–1946), Claude McKay (1890–1948), Alain Locke (1886–1954), Zora Neale Hurston (1891–1960), and James Weldon Johnson (1871–1938).

Beyond the writers

Blues and **jazz** were the musical genres of the Harlem Renaissance, and both had their roots in the black South. Although many African American musicians had been performing for years in small venues, they found themselves suddenly famous after the founding of Okeh's Original Race Records label in 1921. Popular performers included Bessie Smith

Blues and jazz were the musical genres of the Harlem Renaissance. Here, prominent jazz musicians Duke Ellington, seated at the piano, and Louis Armstrong play together in 1946. AP IMAGES

(c. 1894–1937), Ma Rainey (1886–1939), and Mamie Smith (1883–1946). These women used their cultural experiences to infuse meaning into songs. The blues tunes were all about loss of love, personal disaster, and the hardships of life in general.

Jazz followed closely on the heels of the blues, and the first big band (jazz orchestra) was organized in New York City in the early 1920s. The first great jazz soloist was Louis Armstrong (1901–1971), who blew his trumpet first for a smaller band in Chicago, **Illinois**, and then for Fletcher Henderson's (1898–1952) big band in New York in 1924. Other famous jazz musicians included Cab Calloway (1907–1994) and **Duke Ellington** (1899–1974).

There were fewer visual artists in the Harlem Renaissance, and even those who seized the opportunity for growth remain less well known. James Van Der Zee (1886–1983) was a Harlem photographer who had moved from **Massachusetts** in 1905. He was a bold artist and one of the first photographers to consider photography as a form of art. By the 1920s, he had built a successful portrait photography business. It is his work that gives the modern American a glimpse into the African American culture of the Harlem Renaissance.

Sculpture and painting were other artistic mediums that African American artists embraced. Meta Warrick Fuller (1877–1968) became famous for her 1914 sculpture *Ethiopia Awakening*. The piece depicts an African American woman wrapped like a mummy from the waist down, but whose upper torso is living and reaching upward. On her head she wears an Egyptian queen's headdress. The sculpture became a nationalist symbol for African Americans. This and other similar artistic works that reflected African heritage and identity played into white America's sudden interest in black folklore.

Archibald Motley (1891–1981) was an artist who favored oil paints as his medium. Unlike most other important figures of the Harlem Renaissance, he never actually lived in Harlem but claimed Chicago for his home. Motley's paintings documented the African American urban experience, particularly the club scene and nightlife as influenced by the **Roaring Twenties**, or Jazz Age (a period in U.S. history between **World War I** and the **Great Depression** when new forms of social, cultural, and artistic expression were emerging).

Other significant contributions were made in the field of visual arts by painter Aaron Douglas (1898–1979), sculptor Sargent Claude Johnson (1887–1967), and painter Palmer Hayden (1890–1973).

In all art forms, the Harlem Renaissance was a period of development for African American artists. They used their art to express who and what they were as well as were not, where they came from, and where they were going.

Harpers Ferry Raid

John Brown (1800–1859) was an American abolitionist and insurrectionist who planned an all-out war on slavery beginning with a violent raid on the federal arsenal at Harpers Ferry, **Virginia**, in 1859. Brown's unsuccessful raid played a key role in heightening the tensions between the North and South that led to the American **Civil War** (1861–65).

Violence in Kansas

Brown was a militant abolitionist (a person with an aggressive, or warlike, mission to end **slavery**) from **Ohio**. By 1855, his antislavery convictions were so strong he believed that God had chosen him to free the slaves from bondage. He therefore traveled to **Kansas** Territory to join the growing struggle between proslavery and Free Soil forces over the legal status of slavery in Kansas. (The **Free Soil Party** was a U.S. political party with a main objective to prevent the extension of slavery to newly acquired U.S. territories.) Angered by the violent action of proslavery forces in the Free Soil town of Lawrence, Kansas, in May 1856, Brown and four of his sons launched a brutal raid in revenge. In a nighttime attack on a proslavery settlement, Brown and his followers killed five settlers. Learning of his attack, hundreds of settlers rushed to arm themselves. By the end of 1856, at least two hundred Kansans had died.

Brown prepares for war

Brown had long since lost faith in combating slavery by peaceful means, and the trouble in Kansas did not change his mind. He vowed to strike a violent blow at the heart of slavery. In 1857, Brown developed a plan in which he would seize a mountain fortress in Virginia with a small combat force and launch a **slave rebellion**. Once the rebellion had begun, Brown intended to establish an African American republic in the woods of Virginia. From this stronghold, he planned to wage war against the South, his forces continuously strengthened by slave rebellions and private northern assistance.

To that end, Brown began to campaign among the abolitionists in the North. Outwardly, he was seeking money to continue the Free State fight in Kansas. In secret, though, Brown won the support of six prominent antislavery figures who agreed to advise him and raise money for his mission to overthrow slavery. The "Secret Six" was a group of dedicated and well-educated abolitionists and reformers.

Throughout the remainder of 1857, Brown collected and trained a small group of abolitionists in preparation for his mission. In May 1858, Brown held a secret "Constitutional Convention" in Canada attended by a small band of thirty-four blacks and eleven whites. There he outlined his plans to invade Virginia, liberate and arm the slaves, defeat any military force brought against them, organize the blacks into a government, and force the southern states to concede emancipation (freeing the slaves). Under Brown's leadership, the convention approved a constitution for the new state and elected Brown commander in chief of the army.

Brown's proposed invasion was delayed in 1858, when one of his followers partially divulged the plans to several prominent politicians. Brown was forced to go into hiding for a year. It was a disastrous time for postponement. While he waited out the danger, some of the most ardent supporters of his plan lost interest and he lost many of the soldiers he had trained.

The raid

Harpers Ferry, a town in northern Virginia (now located in **West Virginia**), was the site of a federal armory and arsenal (government buildings for storing arms and ammunition). The Harpers Ferry arsenal was the initial target in Brown's plan because he needed weapons to arm the slaves he planned to liberate. On July 3, 1859, Brown set up headquarters at a farm seven miles east of Harpers Ferry. Soon the rest of his twenty-one young recruits (sixteen whites and five blacks) arrived at the headquarters. On the night of October 16, 1859, after several months of refining his plans, Brown led eighteen of his followers on the Harpers Ferry raid. They quickly captured the arsenal, the armory, and a nearby rifle works, and then seized several hostages from the townspeople and surrounding countryside.

Fearing a slave rebellion, the people of Harpers Ferry armed themselves and gathered in the streets. Church bells tolled the alarm over the countryside. Brown stood his ground and anxiously waited for the slaves from the countryside to rally to his cause. Not a single slave arrived. By 11:00 AM the next day, a general battle was in progress between Brown's men, holed up in the small fire engine house of the armory, and the assembled townspeople, farmers, and militia. The raid's fate was sealed when a company of U.S. Marines under the command of army colonel **Robert E. Lee** (1807–1870) charged the engine house. Ten of his men were killed and Brown was wounded and captured.

Brown and his co-conspirators were tried in Virginia rather than by federal authorities, even though their attack had been against federal property. The jury found them guilty of inciting a slave rebellion, murder, and treason against the state of Virginia. After the trial, in a final attempt to save his life, Brown's lawyers collected statements from his friends and relatives alleging that Brown was suffering from insanity. Brown rejected this defense, claiming that he was as sane as anybody. He knew that he could better serve the abolitionist cause as a martyr (someone who suffers or dies for his or her beliefs). He conducted his defense and went to his death with great dignity and conviction, inspiring sympathy among many Northern abolitionists.

Brown's raid on Harpers Ferry intensified the sectional bitterness that led to the American Civil War. The outraged South suspected all Northerners of participating in Brown's crime. In truth, the vast majority of Northerners condemned the incident as the work of a fanatic. The **Republican Party**, the political party that was calling for a stop to the expansion of slavery, had no links with Brown. On the other hand, some Northern abolitionists, including the Secret Six, gathered by the hundreds throughout the North to honor and acclaim Brown's martyrdom. Two years later, Northerners marched to war to the tune of a popular war song called "John Brown's Body."

Benjamin Harrison

Benjamin Harrison was born in 1833 in North Bend, **Ohio**. The grandson of the ninth U.S. president, **William Henry Harrison** (1773–1841; served 1841), Benjamin Harrison became a lawyer and moved to **Indiana**, where he volunteered in **Republican Party** campaigns. Harrison fought in the American **Civil War** (1861–65) as a colonel. When he returned home, he built a reputation as an excellent lawyer.

Harrison served in the U.S. Senate throughout most of the 1880s, where he supported Native Americans and Civil War veterans. In the 1888 presidential campaign, he defended high tariffs (taxes imposed on goods imported from other countries), conservation of wilderness lands, and limited civil service reform. He broke from the traditional Republican viewpoint in his opposition to the Chinese Exclusion Act of 1882, which ended Chinese **immigration** to the United States. (See **Asian Immigration**.)

Harrison was the first candidate to participate in what became known as "front porch speeches." People would visit him at his home in Indiana and listen to him speak from his front porch. This campaign style encouraged citizens to think of Harrison as one of them, a regular man with a regular home and family. These speeches were not as informal as they appeared; Harrison's campaign managers carefully selected which newspaper reporters and community members would attend.

Harrison beat his opponent, President **Grover Cleveland** (1837–1908; served 1885–89 and 1893–97). A Republican president was back in office, and for the first time in years, the Republican Party dominated both the **executive branch** and **legislative branch** of the federal government.

In the White House

Harrison was not a unique leader, but his administration was efficient and productive. Some of the legislation that passed during his presidency had a major impact on American business. Harrison supported the McKinley Tariff of 1890, a law that raised tariff rates an average of 49.5 percent. The bill also gave the president expanded powers in the area of foreign trade.

The American public hated giant corporations and big businesses that took over the economy and forced consumers into paying high fees and prices. Republicans and Democrats alike rallied together in the call for reform of dishonest business practices such as **monopolies**. (Monopolies are businesses that have total control over a certain sector of the economy, including prices; in a monopoly, there is no competition.) As a result of this public outcry, the Harrison administration supported and passed the **Sherman Antitrust Act** of 1890. This act was the first federal law to regulate big business. The Sherman Antitrust Act made it a federal crime for businesses to form trusts (the concept of several companies banding together to form an organization that limits competition by controlling the production and distribution of a product or service). Although it had flaws, it was an important first step.

Another important piece of legislation passed during Harrison's term was the Sherman Silver Purchase Act of 1890. This bill had the U.S. Treasury purchase 4.5 million ounces of silver at market price each month. The silver was bought with treasury notes that could be redeemed in either gold or silver. Holders of these notes were so eager to turn them in for gold (because they received more money per note that way) that they nearly emptied the Treasury's supply. The act increased the production of silver, which sent silver prices down rather than up, and that was the intent. The act was repealed in 1893, the year of the worst economic decline the United States had ever experienced. Historians point to several factors that contributed to the **Panic of 1893**, including the Sherman Silver Purchase Act. In addition to the depletion of the nation's gold reserves and the decrease in silver prices, railroads went bankrupt and banks across the country began to fail. The result was high unemployment and a severe shortage of money circulating in the economy.

Harrison's foreign policy Harrison was one of the most active presidents in the area of foreign diplomacy. He took the United States to the brink of war with Chile over an incident involving American sailors who were harmed in the port city of Valparaiso. After discussion between the countries' leaders, Chile apologized and paid the United States $75,000 for the incident.

In 1889, the president called the first modern Pan-American Conference in **Washington, D.C.** Leaders from North, Central, and South America attended the conference in an effort to develop military, economic, social, political, and commercial cooperation between the three Americas. Conference attendees developed treaties on how to resolve international conflicts and revised tariff levels. In addition, an organization that would eventually be known as the Pan-American Union was established. The union offered technical and informational services to the Americas and provided a safe place for official documents. By forming various councils, the union took on the responsibility for furthering cooperative relations throughout the Americas. Its founding is celebrated on Pan-American Day each year in April.

As successful as he was in other foreign endeavors, Harrison did not achieve his goal where **Hawaii** was concerned. Harrison was in favor of annexing (adding another U.S. territory) Hawaii, but he was unable to convince the Senate to do so. Still, because of his efforts and because Hawaii did eventually become part of the United States, modern historians credit Harrison and his administration for putting the United States on its path to becoming an empire.

Harrison's popularity wanes Harrison's popularity among the public took a severe blow on three national issues. The first was his support of the McKinley Tariff. Millions of citizens lost trust in a president who seemed to be siding more with big-business interests than with the average working man. The second issue involved the dissatisfaction of farmers—those hardest hit by the depression—in the South and West. Harrison had done virtually nothing to improve the farmers' situation, so he lost their support. Finally, a series of violent labor strikes linked

Harrison to monopoly industrialists and bankers. Voters did not feel represented in the White House.

Furthermore, Harrison passed a great deal of Republican legislation in his first year in office. Because of the amount of money Congress spent, it soon became known as the "Billion Dollar" Congress.

Harrison could not undo the damage his image had suffered. He had never been known publicly as an overly friendly man, yet he put his family at the center of his life. (In fact, Harrison's campaign activities in 1892 were very minimal due to the illness of first lady Caroline Harrison. She died two weeks before the election.) Harrison's tendency to be a private man, coupled with the unpopular events throughout his term, led him directly out of the White House. Grover Cleveland was re-elected in the 1892 election. Upon learning of his defeat, Harrison told his family he felt like he had been freed from prison. He died in 1901.

William Henry Harrison

William Henry Harrison attained national recognition at an early age for his military victory over Shawnee leader Tecumseh (1768–1813) at the Battle of Tippecanoe in 1811. He enjoyed a long political career before winning the presidential election of 1840, but he died soon after taking office as the ninth president.

Harrison was born on February 9, 1773, in **Virginia** into one of the state's leading families. His father had been one of the signers of the **Declaration of Independence**. Young Harrison briefly studied medicine before joining the U.S. **Army** in 1791. In 1795, Harrison married Anna Symmes; together they would have ten children. A grandson, **Benjamin Harrison** (1833–1901; served 1889–93), would become president of the United States in 1889.

Harrison served in campaigns against the Indians in the Northwest Territory (the early U.S. region including lands that would become **Ohio**, **Indiana**, **Michigan**, **Illinois**, **Wisconsin**, and part of **Minnesota**) for seven years. In 1799, Harrison, an avid spokesman for **westward expansion**, became the Northwest Territory's first delegate to Congress.

Harrison was soon appointed governor of the newly created Indiana Territory. He had the nearly impossible mission of winning the trust of Native Americans while at the same time acquiring as much of their land as he could for the government. In 1809, he negotiated a treaty that transferred almost 2.9 million acres to the United States, bringing tensions between Native Americans and white settlers to a boiling point.

Around that time, Tecumseh developed the idea of a confederation of all Indian tribes to fight against U.S. invasion of their lands. His brother, Tenskwatawa (c. 1768–1834), founded a religious movement that preached a return to traditional Indian values and a rejection of the ways of the white man. Together, **Tecumseh and Tenskwatawa**, also known as the Shawnee Prophet, drew a large group of followers from various tribes. These followers settled in a village called Prophetstown, ready to fight for their land.

Battle of Tippecanoe

As Harrison continued to seek Indian lands for the government, Tecumseh's resistance became an obstacle. In 1811, Harrison marched about one thousand soldiers to a camp near Prophetstown; Tecumseh was away at the time. Early on the morning of November 7, Prophetstown warriors launched a surprise attack against Harrison's troops. Harrison's forces beat back the attackers. He was able to take possession of their settlement, but 188 of his men were killed or wounded in the process and a few months later the Indians returned to their village. Some viewed Harrison as a hero, but others questioned his victory as an incomplete job.

Commander in War of 1812

During the **War of 1812**, a conflict over trading between England and the United States, Harrison served in several military positions, including supreme commander of the Army of the Northwest. After many difficult battles, he led the victorious Battle of the Thames in 1813 near Chatham, Ontario, where Tecumseh was killed in battle. Once again, he received a hero's welcome by some, but others criticized his military performance. In May 1814, he resigned from the army and moved to a farm in Ohio. Between 1816 and 1829 Harrison served as a congressman, senator, and U.S. minister to Colombia.

"Tippecanoe and Tyler too"

During the 1830s, there was a growing reaction against the alleged abuse of power by President **Andrew Jackson** (1767–1845; served 1829–37) in the **Democratic Party**. In response, a mixed group of politicians and others formed the **Whig Party**. Harrison became the Whig candidate for the presidential nomination in 1840. He was nominated as a military hero and a spokesman for development of the West.

The Whigs did not offer a real political platform, only a pledge to correct the abuses of the current administration. Whig strategists created a winning campaign by portraying Harrison (widely known as "Old Tippecanoe") as a man of the people. They waged the first modern presidential campaign by selling souvenirs, distributing campaign materials, flooding the country with speakers, and using songs, slogans, and verses. The most famous cry was "Tippecanoe and Tyler too." (**John Tyler** [1790–1862] was Harrison's running mate.) Harrison won the election with ease.

Inauguration day was chilly and rainy, and the new president caught a cold that quickly developed into pneumonia. On April 4, 1841, after only one month in office, Harrison died in the White House.

Hawaii

Hawaii was the last state to join the Union when it was admitted on August 21, 1959. It is actually a group of 132 islands situated in the northern Pacific Ocean, about 2,400 miles (3,862 kilometers) westsouthwest of San Francisco, **California**. The four largest islands of the state are Hawaii, Maui, Oahu, and Kauai.

English explorer James Cook (1728–1779) first sighted Oahu in 1778. At that time, a chief ruled each Hawaiian island. Once Europeans began sailing to the islands, the native populations were exposed to smallpox, venereal disease, liquor, and firearms. Hawaii's first written constitution was adopted in 1840. In 1848, a land reform called the Great Mahele fostered the expansion of sugar plantations, and subsequent decades saw the arrival of Chinese laborers to work those plantations.

In 1893, Hawaii's queen was overthrown during an American-led revolution. Soon after, Hawaii's government adopted a new constitution and was proclaimed the Republic of Hawaii. The **Spanish-American War** in 1898 fed expansionist (desire to expand territorial holdings) sentiment in the United States. Hawaii was a prime military asset, and its profitable sugar plantations were attractive. In June 1900, Hawaii became a territory of the United States.

In 2006, Hawaii, also known as the Aloha state, was home to nearly 1.3 million people, 24.9 percent of whom were white. Another 2 percent were African American, and 42 percent were Asian. Only 8.5 percent were Pacific Islanders or **Native Hawaiians**.

Hawaii's economy is based on tourism and defense, though in recent years, the state has become increasingly important as an economic, educational, and cultural bridge between the United States and Asia and the Pacific. The **Iraq Invasion** (2003–) and the subsequent recession had a serious impact on the state's tourism industry. One month after the war began in March 2003, Hawaii's tourism business decreased by one-third. During a wartime economy, it is not unusual for people to be more frugal with their money. This thriftiness hurts states that rely on tourism for their revenue.

Hawaii is one of the most expensive states in which to live, as it is the second among the fifty states in terms of personal taxes. As of 2006, it had nine individual income tax brackets, ranging from 1.4 percent to 8.25 percent. It is the only state to have a single, unified public school system, which was founded in 1840.

Unlike other states, the main modes of transportation in Hawaii are airplanes and helicopters. In 2005, Hawaii had thirty-one airports and seventeen heliports. It has two railroads, but only 12.5 miles (20 kilometers) of track.

Rutherford B. Hayes

U.S. president Rutherford B. Hayes was the victor in one of the most fiercely fought elections in American history.

Hayes was born on October 4, 1822. He was the youngest of five children born to Rutherford and Sophia Hayes in Delaware, **Ohio**. His father died before Hayes's birth, and his uncle became his guardian. Hayes graduated from Kenyon College in 1842. Three years later, he graduated with a law degree from Harvard. After college, he practiced law in Fremont, Ohio, before moving to Cincinnati, Ohio, in 1849, where he eventually took a job as city solicitor (a position equal to a modern district attorney).

Hayes married Lucy Webb in 1852, and the couple had eight children.

From soldier to politician

Hayes fought in the American **Civil War** (1861–65) and was wounded in battle. While still in the army, he was nominated by the **Republican Party** to serve in Congress. Hayes accepted the nomination but refused to campaign, citing his obligation to fight for his country as his number one priority. Even without a campaign, he won a seat in the Thirty-ninth Congress and another in the Fortieth. He resigned from his position in 1867 to run for governor of Ohio. He was victorious and served from 1868 to 1872 and again from 1876 to 1877.

Hayes's war record and reputation as a loyal Republican made him a popular presidential nominee for the 1876 election. He ran against **New York** governor Samuel Tilden (1814–1886). Toward the end of the campaign, Tilden was expected to win. Hayes himself believed his opponent would be the next president of the United States. More registered voters participated in the 1876 presidential election than ever before: 81.8 percent.

Military man and politician Rutherford B. Hayes won a heated election to become president against the favored Democratic candidate Samuel Tilden. THE LIBRARY OF CONGRESS

In a U.S. presidential election, there are two kinds of votes: popular (total number of votes by individuals) and electoral (assigned to states based on population; the higher the population count, the more electoral votes that state is worth). After all votes had been counted, Tilden clearly won the popular vote. But the electoral votes from **Florida**, **Louisiana**, **South Carolina**, and **Oregon** were in dispute. A congressional committee was formed to investigate the situation. That committee included five **Supreme Court** justices, five members from the House of Representatives, and five senators.

The plan was to have seven Democrats, seven Republicans, and one independent. The independent was Supreme Court associate justice David Davis (1815–1886). However, he happened to be elected a U.S. senator and thus could not serve on the committee. His replacement was a Republican, so every vote the committee took after reviewing the evidence resulted in an 8–7 split in favor of Hayes. That resulted in Hayes being awarded all the electoral votes and, therefore, the victory.

In office

Tilden was disappointed but did not dispute the findings. He believed the United States needed to move on. Hayes's years in office were uneventful compared to the conflict under which he entered. He had hoped to overturn the patronage system that controlled the government, but he was unable to do so. The patronage system was an unethical means of controlling bureaucracy in which wealthy men were appointed certain government positions in return for their vote. This put a lot of unqualified, dishonest men in powerful positions and made government ineffective on many levels. Hayes recognized he could not change the way things were, but he refused to participate in the system. Instead, he chose his administration based on individual merit and ability. This served only to turn his fellow Republicans against him.

Hayes promised protection to the African Americans of the war-torn South. At the same time, he encouraged the states to return to a more honest, peaceful way of governing. Despite the victory of the North in the Civil War, the South's attitude toward **slavery** and African Americans had not changed much. They resented being told how to live their lives, and troops from the **Confederate States of America** (the group of states that were part of **secession** from the United States) had been sent to watch over the South as **Reconstruction** (efforts to rebuild the nation following the Civil War) began. Hayes removed the troops in 1877, essentially ending the period of Reconstruction.

That same year, Hayes was faced with the first nationwide labor strike. Railroad workers had been forced to take pay cuts beginning in 1873. By 1877, they went on strike in hopes of ending the unjust treatment. Hayes sent in federal troops to control the strikes that were erupting throughout the states. In doing so, he ushered in an era when state and federal forces sided with companies against aggravated laborers.

Does not seek reelection

Hayes promised not to seek reelection, and he kept that promise. He was succeeded by another Ohio Republican, former U.S. representative **James A. Garfield** (1831–1881; served 1881). Hayes lived out his life in retirement at his family estate, Spiegel Grove, in Fremont, and died in 1893.

William Randolph Hearst

William Randolph Hearst is best remembered as the father of yellow journalism, a type of reporting that focused on sensationalism to sell newspapers and magazines. (See **News Media**.)

Hearst was born on April 29, 1863, to a U.S. senator and his school-teacher wife. Young Hearst attended an elite New England prep school, St. Paul's, and went on extensive tours of Europe. He was accepted into Harvard University, where he studied for two years before being expelled for misconduct.

Hearst's father acquired the financially failing *San Francisco Examiner* in 1880. He gave his son ownership of the newspaper in 1887. The younger Hearst hired the best writers of the era and paid them top wages to write reports of events that never happened. He soon discovered that stories on crime, sex, scandal, and sports sell newspapers; reporting actual facts did not really seem to matter.

Broadens his horizons

Using a $7.5 million gift from his mother, Hearst moved his operations to New York City in 1895 and bought the failing *New York Morning Journal*. Using the same unethical reporting techniques that brought him success in the recent past, Hearst brought circulation of the newspaper up from seventy-seven thousand to more than one million within a year. Through yellow journalism, Hearst's personal fortune grew exponentially. In 1898, Hearst papers published many sensational articles about the **Spanish-American War.** Hearst and a group of writers and artists reported directly from the battle lines.

By the time Hearst married Millicent Willson in 1903, he had established two new newspapers: the *Chicago American* and the *Chicago Examiner*. His wife was just twenty-one years old when she married the forty-year-old publisher. They eventually had five sons. In 1917, Hearst began a romantic relationship with twenty-year-old actress Marion Davies (1897–1961). It was an affair that would last until his death.

In 1904, Hearst added the *Boston American* and the *Los Angeles Examiner* to his empire. By this time, he was buying newspapers not only to expand his wealth, but also to control the news in an attempt to further his political ambitions. Hearst dreamed of being president of the

United States. Although in 1902 and 1904 he won a Democratic seat in Congress as a U.S. representative from **New York**, he was not an effective congressman. He rarely showed up for his congressional duties, and his absenteeism cost him his political career.

Life goes on

By 1935, Hearst owned twenty-six daily newspapers and eleven Sunday editions in nineteen cities across the country. He claimed nearly 14 percent of the total U.S. daily circulation. In addition, he owned the International News Service and the King Features syndication service. Newspapers were not his only interest. Hearst owned six magazines, including the popular *Good Housekeeping* and *Cosmopolitan*. His investments extended to radio and Hollywood, and he owned over $50 million in New York real estate. Aside from his castle in San Simeon, **California** (worth $37 million), Hearst owned homes throughout the nation and decorated them with his art collection, the largest ever assembled by one person.

By the time Hearst died in 1951, he owned just eight newspapers. The hardship of the **Great Depression** (1929–41; a period of depressed economy and high unemployment) forced him to give up much of his empire. Hearst's sons continued their father's newspaper business, but worked to rid the family name of the bad reputation it had earned. They set up the Hearst Foundation, which continues in the twenty-first century to give scholarships to journalism students.

Ernest Hemingway

Ernest Hemingway is praised as one of the greatest American writers of the twentieth century. With an understated prose style, his fiction features a narrow range of characters and a harsh focus on violence and machismo (an exaggerated sense of masculine toughness). Many critics and readers have come to appreciate the depth of the author's vision beneath his tough-guy restraint.

Early years

Born on July 21, 1899, Hemingway led a fairly happy, upper-middle-class childhood in Oak Park, **Illinois**. By his teens, he had become interested in literature, and he wrote a weekly column for his high school newspaper and contributed poems and stories to the school magazine.

Upon graduation in 1917, Hemingway became a junior reporter for the *Kansas City Star,* covering the police and hospital beats and writing feature stories. He quickly demonstrated a talent for the kind of powerful, unbiased stories of violence and despair that later dominated his fiction.

Drives ambulance in World War I

Hemingway tried to join the U.S. **Army** during **World War I** (1914–18), but his poor eyesight prevented it. Instead, he volunteered as an ambulance driver in Italy for the **American Red Cross**. He was badly wounded in both legs by a shrapnel explosion on the Italian battlefront. While he was recovering, he fell in love with an American nurse, who abruptly left him. This experience later provided the basis of his novel *A Farewell to Arms* (1929).

Back home after the war, Hemingway drafted stories drawn from his boyhood years and wartime experiences that captured his awakening sense of life's misfortunes. He eventually returned to journalism to support himself, contributing features to the *Toronto (Ontario) Star.*

Expatriate in Paris

Following his first marriage (there were four in all) in 1921, Hemingway moved to Paris, the literary capital of Europe in the 1920s. He traveled frequently, covering the Greco-Turkish War of 1922 and writing special-interest pieces for the Toronto paper. During this period, Hemingway matured as a writer, greatly aided in his artistic development by his close contact in Paris with prominent writers of the time, many who were also expatriates, or people who live outside their own country. They included American fiction writer Gertrude Stein (1874–1946), Irish fiction writer James Joyce (1882–1941), and American fiction writer **F. Scott Fitzgerald** (1896–1940).

In 1924, Hemingway published a series of eighteen sketches stemming from his war experiences combined with a group of short stories, calling it *In Our Time.* The majority of the stories focus on Nick Adams, the perfect example of a Hemingway hero. The early stories introduce Nick as a vulnerable adolescent attempting to understand a violent and confusing world. On the surface, Nick appears tough and insensitive. Most critics believe that the toughness of the Hemingway hero masks a deep and sensitive knowledge of tragedy surrounding him. The short stories in the work are considered some of Hemingway's finest efforts.

Two novels

Hemingway returned to the United States in 1926, the year his novel *The Sun Also Rises* was published. The novel is about a group of American and English expatriates in Paris, all of whom have suffered physically and emotionally during World War I. The narrator is Jake Barnes, who was badly wounded in the war. In his postwar life, he establishes his own code of behavior, no longer believing in the dictates of society. He engages in a doomed love affair with the alcoholic Lady Brett Ashley. He is unable to have sexual relations because of his war wounds and stands by as Brett Ashley goes through a series of lovers.

Upon its release, critics objected to *The Sun Also Rises* as a story of meaningless drinking and sex. But a few critics immediately recognized the novel as a literary work and praised its quest for meaning and values that could endure even in a modern world in which traditional values have lost their force.

In 1927, Hemingway moved to Key West, **Florida**, where he could indulge his love of fishing and work on *A Farewell to Arms*. The story of a love affair between an American soldier and an English nurse, the novel expresses the Hemingway code of toughness and endurance in a violent age. Following the novel's immense success, Hemingway was recognized as a major force in literature.

The tough guy

In the early 1930s, Hemingway contributed a series of articles to a new magazine, *Esquire*. In these articles, intentionally or not, he projected an image of himself as a man's man—tough and foulmouthed, an outdoorsman and also a notorious playboy. True to that image, he took up fishing from his cabin cruiser *Pilar* in the wealthy playground of the Bahamas. One product of this time was the novel *To Have and Have Not* (1937), which dramatized his admiration for a Key West desperado named Harry Morgan.

When the Spanish Civil War broke out in 1936, Hemingway wanted to play a role in the fight against fascism (an authoritarian political system in which individual liberty is suppressed for the interests of the state). He sailed for Spain in 1937 under contract to the North American Newspaper Alliance (NANA). His Spanish Civil War novel *For Whom the Bell Tolls* was published in 1940. The novel portrays modern war in all its horror. It was the most commercially successful of Hemingway's books through 1940.

The 1940s and 1950s

After the start of **World War II** (1939–45), Hemingway again became personally involved. He set up an organization to spy on German Nazi agents who were gathering in Cuba. He even supervised the adaptation of his beloved fishing boat, *Pilar,* to be used against German submarines in the Caribbean. He spent part of the war in England and France and took part in efforts to liberate France from German occupation.

In 1952, after a long unproductive period, Hemingway published *The Old Man and the Sea,* a novella based on a true story he had heard from a Cuban boatman. The tale of old Santiago and his battle with the giant marlin was a kind of universal fable: one man alone, locked in a struggle with a worthy adversary. Though the old man eventually lost his prize to sharks, he had carried on against great odds with courage and endurance, the qualities that Hemingway most revered. The novella earned Hemingway a Pulitzer Prize in 1953.

Hemingway won the Nobel Prize for literature in 1954, but he had been badly hurt in a plane accident and could not attend the ceremony. Other physical ailments began to limit his creative energy. In the fall and winter of 1957–58, Hemingway summoned energy to write a series of sketches on his life in Paris from 1921 to 1926. Eventually named *A Moveable Feast* (1964), it is considered the best work of his later life.

In 1960, Hemingway suffered a serious mental breakdown. His depressive behavior and other illnesses persisted, and he committed suicide the following year.

Lasting reputation

During his lifetime, Hemingway actively promoted his larger-than-life reputation as a tough American hero who sought to experience violence as well as write about it. He was an expert in the arenas of war, bullfighting, deep-sea fishing, boxing, big-game hunting, and reckless, extravagant living—experiences that he often recounted in his fiction. Yet

Hemingway viewed writing as his sacred occupation. He tried to be painfully honest in his writing, seeking new truths while distancing himself from traditions that were no longer meaningful. His spare prose allows his readers to make their own judgments about the complex and jaded world he portrays.

Patrick Henry

Patrick Henry was a Virginian who advocated colonial rebellion against Great Britain. He had a successful law practice and served in public office as both a legislator and as governor of **Virginia**. Remembered for the phrase "Give me liberty or give me death," Henry had a talent for oratory that inspired the birth of a nation.

Early life

Henry was born in Studley, Virginia, in a western county of the colony on May 29, 1736. He was the second son of Colonel John Henry and Sarah Winston. John Henry was from Scotland and had an education from Aberdeen University that served him in educating his own children.

Henry learned to read and write in school. From his father, he learned some Latin and Greek as well as mathematics and history. Growing up in rural Virginia, inland from the coastal tidewater region, Henry spent much of his time hunting.

Henry's family could not afford to send him to college. Many middle-class children in Virginia were expected to learn a practical trade instead. When Henry was fifteen, he began a yearlong apprenticeship as a clerk in a country store. In 1752, John Henry bought goods so Patrick and his older brother William could open their own store, but the business failed.

Marriage and law

Patrick Henry married sixteen-year-old Sarah Shelton in 1754. Together they would have six children. Sarah's father gave the Henrys a 300-acre farm and six slaves. Henry tried tobacco farming for a couple years until a fire destroyed their house. After that Henry opened another shop and, when that failed, worked as a bartender in his father-in-law's tavern in Hanover County.

In 1760, Henry decided to study law to improve his earning power. Within a year, he passed oral examinations in Williamsburg, the provincial capital, and received a license to practice law.

Henry handled a case in 1763 that helped make his career as a lawyer and politician. The Privy Council in Great Britain, which reviewed colonial laws, had struck down a Virginia law regarding the salaries of Anglican ministers. In a case involving the application of that law, Henry argued that by striking down a duly passed law of the colony, the crown in England had violated the rights of the colonists to govern themselves concerning local matters. Great Britain's refusal to approve local laws later became the first in the list of complaints against King George III (1738–1820) in the **Declaration of Independence**.

Politics

Henry became a legislator in the **House of Burgesses**, the colonial legislature in Virginia, in 1765. Great Britain had recently passed the **Stamp Act** for the colonies. The Stamp Act imposed business taxes that were normally regulated by local laws and was very unpopular among colonial merchants.

In late May, just weeks after entering the House of Burgesses, Henry introduced a series of resolutions against the Stamp Act. The resolutions condemned taxation without representation. Henry said that people have a natural right to govern themselves and a right to disobey laws imposed on them without their consent. Four of the seven resolves passed, and Henry became known throughout the colonies an a spokesman for American freedom.

As the American colonies began to organize against Great Britain, Henry served on the First and Second Continental Congresses in 1774 and 1775. (See **Continental Congress, First** and **Continental Congress, Second**.) Most of his public service, however, was at the state level in Virginia. When Virginia wrote a constitution in 1776, Henry became the first governor of the state, a position he held until 1779 and again from 1784 to 1786.

In 1787, the American states sent delegates to a federal convention in Philadelphia, **Pennsylvania**. Its task was to rewrite the **Articles of Confederation**, but instead it wrote a whole new document, the **Constitution** of the United States of America. Henry declined to serve at the convention because he disapproved of the plan to form a strong

Patrick Henry's Stamp Act Resolves

Resolves of the House of Burgesses in Virginia, June 1765.

That the first Adventurers & Settlers of this his Majesty's Colony and Dominion of Virginia, brought with them, and transmitted to their Posterity, and all other his Majesty's Subjects since inhabiting in this his Majesty's Colony, all the Liberties, Privileges, Franchises, and Immunities, that at any Time have been held, enjoyed, and possessed, by the People of Great Britain.

That by Two Royal Charters, granted by King James the First, the Colonies aforesaid are Declared Entitled, to all Liberties, Privileges and Immunities, of Denizens and Natural Subjects (to all Intents and Purposes) as if they had been Abiding and Born within the Realm of England.

That the Taxation of the People by Themselves, or by Persons Chosen by Themselves to Represent them, who can only know what Taxes the People are able to bear, or the easiest Method of Raising them, and must themselves be affected by every Tax laid upon the People, is the only Security against a Burthensome Taxation; and the Distinguishing Characteristic of British freedom; and, without which, the ancient Constitution cannot exist.

That his Majesty's Liege People of this his most Ancient and Loyal Colony, have, without Interruption, the inestimable Right of being Governed by such Laws, respecting their internal Polity and Taxation, as are derived from their own Consent, with the Approbation of their Sovereign, or his Substitute; which Right hath never been Forfeited, or Yielded up; but hath been constantly recognized by the Kings and People of Great Britain.

Resolved therefore, That the General Assembly of this Colony, with the Consent of his Majesty, or his Substitute, Have the Sole Right and Authority to lay Taxes and Impositions upon It's [sic] Inhabitants: And, That every Attempt to vest such Authority in any other Person or Persons whatsoever, has a Manifest Tendency to Destroy American Freedom.

That his Majesty's Liege People, Inhabitants of this Colony, are not bound to yield Obedience to any Law or Ordinance whatsoever, designed to impose any Taxation upon them, other than the Laws or Ordinances of the General Assembly as aforesaid.

That any Person who shall, by Speaking, or Writing, assert or maintain, That any Person or Persons, other than the General Assembly of this Colony, with such Consent as aforesaid, have any Right or Authority to lay or impose any Tax whatever on the Inhabitants thereof, shall be Deemed, an Enemy to this his Majesty's Colony.

federal government. He did serve, however, in the Virginia convention that had to decide whether to approve the Constitution. Henry was a leading spokesman against approval because he thought the federal government would be too strong and that the Constitution did not contain enough protection for individual liberty. Henry worked to make **James Madison** (1751–1836), who became known as the Father of the Constitution, and others agree to add a **Bill of Rights** to the Constitution in exchange for approval.

Later years

Public service had been financially costly to Henry, so he resumed his law practice in 1788. By his death, he had amassed a small fortune in land holdings. He was elected to a sixth term as governor of Virginia in 1796, but he declined to serve. In 1799, former president **George Washington** (1732–1799; served 1789–97) convinced Henry to serve again in the state legislature. This time Henry agreed, but he died on June 6, 1799, before his term began.

Highways

Automobiles became an integral part of U.S. culture in the 1920s. There were about 3 million miles of road in the nation at the start of the decade, but only 36,000 of those miles were paved. As more and more cars and trucks used the roads, it became clear that the dirt paths originally built for horses were not going to serve the needs of Americans with vehicles.

To help create and maintain interstate highways, the Federal Highway Act was passed in 1921. The law provided federal funding for the highway system. It was agreed that highways running east to west would be labeled with even numbers, and those running north to south with odd numbers.

More than 10,000 miles of road were being paved annually by 1929, making traveling easier than ever. Family vacations became popular and led to the establishment of "car camps"—early motels that offered bathrooms facilities and tents for weary travelers. Along with these camps came roadside diners and gas stations.

In 1943, the National Interregional Highway Committee recommended a 39,000-mile interregional highway system, with a focus on how such a transportation network would influence urban development.

The Federal Aid Highway Act of 1944 authorized a 40,000-mile interstate highway system connecting major metropolitan areas and industrial centers. Construction was slow, as funding was scarce at the end of

World War II (1939–45) and states were in no hurry to divert funds from other projects. The 1952 Federal-Aid Highway Act was the first law to specifically designate federal funds for highway construction. Under the act, a total of $25 million would go to the states if they would match those funds equally. By 1953, states had constructed nearly 20 percent of the designated interstate highway system. Little of it was of suitable quality.

President **Dwight D. Eisenhower** (1890–1969; served 1953–61) liked the idea of an interstate highway system. In 1954, Congress passed another Federal-Aid Highway Act, this time authorizing $175 million for a program that would have the federal government funding 60 percent and the states funding 40 percent. When that still did not provide adequate funding for the roads, Congress passed the Highway Act in 1956.

The 1956 act called for a thirteen-year project that would result in a 40,300-mile national highway system. Ninety percent of the cost would come from the federal government, and individual states would be responsible for maintenance costs of their sections of the highways. To avoid amassing huge debts, Congress created a pay-as-you-go program. Taxes on gasoline and on truck use, including tire and equipment sales, established the basis for funding. These taxes went directly to the government and were reimbursed through consumers' purchases the next year. The tax revenue raised more than enough for the federal portion of construction expenses each year.

The Highway Act provided more than $1 billion to begin highway construction and was considered one of the greatest public works programs in American history. By the mid-1990s, more than 40,000 miles of the interstate system had been built at a cost of $137 billion. The system covers all fifty states as well as the Commonwealth of Puerto Rico.

Hip-hop and Rap Music

Hip-hop began in the 1970s in New York City's South Bronx neighborhood as a street-born cultural movement based on four pillars: DJ-ing, MC-ing (later known as rap), breakdancing, and graffiti art. By the 1980s, hip-hop was the primary cultural movement of the African American and Hispanic communities. Mainstream white consumers quickly accepted hip-hop through movies, music videos, radio play, and media coverage. Rap, in particular, found a wide multicultural audience and emerged as one of the most original forms of music in the late twentieth century.

Early rap and hip-hop musicians such as LL Cool J (1968–) and the group Run-DMC spread the sound from **New York** to **California**. Run-DMC formed in 1982 and watched its first record become the first rap-music gold album in 1983. MC Hammer (1962–) and Vanilla Ice (1967–) gave rap music a home on the pop charts, and by the 1990s rap had left the inner city and branched into many different divisions. Popular cable television station MTV aided the phenomenon by airing music videos and gaving artists another means of spreading their music and image. Tone Loc (1966–), LL Cool J, Queen Latifah (1970–), and Salt-N-Pepa appeared on the Top 40 charts.

West Coast Gangsta rap emerged in the early 1990s. Gangsta rappers wanted to return the music to its roots: the streets. Dr. Dre (1965–), N.W.A., and Ice Cube (1969–) sang of the violence of living in the ghetto (impoverished inner-city areas). Unlike early hard-core rap, gangsta rap had crossover appeal. Snoop Doggy Dogg (1971–) was one example of a rapper who could establish a following without concern for cultural and racial differences. His debut album in 1993 entered the pop charts in the number-one slot. Gangsta rap became the main genre of the early 1990s, and the more it sang of guns and drugs, the more popular it was among white teen audiences in the suburbs. Parents and special interest groups lobbied for stronger restrictions as gangsta rap's explicit lyrics filled suburban homes across the nation.

The East Coast was home to a different hip-hop sound. Afrocentric groups like Jungle Brothers and De La Soul brought a jazzy, intellectual quality to rap music as they focused their lyrics on black history and thought. Unlike the West Coast sound, the East Coast sound remained largely underground and never had the commercial impact of its cousin.

The last half of the 1990s found musicians concerned with holding on to the roots of hip-hop culture. Recording stars like the Black Eyed Peas brought back the original sounds of hip-hop that had made it so popular in the 1970s. True hip-hop musicians criticized hard rap performers like Sean "Puffy" Combs (1969–) for selling out and preferring commercial success to cultural commitment. The feud between East and West Coast styles escalated to violence. Both Tupac Shakur (1971–1996) and The Notorious B.I.G. (also known as Biggie Smalls) (1972–1997)—two of the decade's most popular rap artists—were murdered.

Some earlier rappers like Run-DMC wanted to be role models for African American youth and decried gang involvement while actively

Run-DMC formed in 1982, spread the hip-hop/rap sound across the country, and their record "Run-DMC" became the first rap-music gold album. AP IMAGES

participating in social causes. Queen Latifah and others spoke out against drugs. Others, like Shakur and Smalls, chose to sing about the ugly reality of poverty, drugs, violence, and life on the streets.

The first decade of the twenty-first century focused the spotlight on artists who successfully combined the earlier hip-hop sound with the more hard-core rap. Marshall Mathers (1972–), better known as Eminem and Slim Shady, was one of the highest-selling musicians of that decade. In fact, he was one of the highest-selling rap musicians in history. His albums sold over seventy million copies worldwide by 2007, and he won several Grammy Awards. Although critics have praised Eminem for his energy, as well as for sparking public interest in poetry, he has also been denounced for his lyrics, which some say promote violence and homophobia (fear of homosexuals) as well as misogyny (hatred of women). Eminem defies labels, as his music has been categorized as a combination of hip-hop, Gangsta rap, and even pop.

Hollywood Blacklisting

Americans spent the 1930s trying to survive the **Great Depression**. Many people lost faith in their country's economic system, and some turned to **communism**, an economic theory in which the production and distribution of products and services are owned and controlled by the government. It was a low point in American history.

After **World War II** (1939–45), America entered into a **"cold war"** with Russia. This was not an actual war but a time of intense tension and competition between the two countries. Russia was communist, and America feared communism and the possibility that it might spread. (See also **Red Scare**.)

In 1947, a congressional committee known as the **House Un-American Activities Committee** (HUAC) began investigating the motion picture industry for communist influence. The **movie** industry was made up of idealistic writers, actors, and producers; many had been against the war and dismayed with the leadership in place at the White House. Some had joined the American Communist Party, which boasted a membership of around fifty thousand during the war.

Going to movie theaters was a major pastime in America during the mid-twentieth century. Films provided a brief escape from the worries of the day, and even those families who did not have much money could enjoy an occasional movie. Films had great influence, and the government knew this. The investigation into the film industry began when it was alleged that communist values were being glorified in movies.

A witness list of about forty people was prepared. For one reason or another, only eleven of these individuals were called before the committee to testify. Most of these professionals were screenwriters. The question put before them was: "Are you now, or have you ever been, a member of the Communisty Party?" Just one witness, playwright Bertolt Brecht (1898–1956), answered. It immediately became clear that answering that one question was not enough to satisfy the HUAC; it wanted names of other members. Ultimately, it wanted to embarrass the witnesses by forcing them to publicly tell on their friends and colleagues.

Ten of the original witnesses refused to answer the question, not necessarily because they were members of the Communist Party but because they believed that political affiliation in the United States was a private issue. Refusing to answer, however, could be construed as an admission of "guilt." These ten screenwriters became known as the Hollywood Ten, and their names were added to a list that circulated throughout the industry. Anyone on that list could no longer work in the movie industry. The Ten each served a one-year jail sentence.

By the end of the investigation, about three hundred entertainers were blacklisted; only about thirty were able to rebuild their careers. Some continued to work infrequently, but only if they agreed to use false names or not receive credit for their work. The blacklisting went beyond the professional realm, however, and severed even the closest of friendships. Families were destroyed in some cases where both spouses worked in the industry and one gave the name of the other.

Blacklisting continued until 1957 despite the fact that evidence of the promotion of communist values in film was virtually nonexistent.

Holocaust

During **World War II** (1939–45), the leader of Germany, Adolf Hitler (1889–1945), created a program of ethnic cleansing that came to be called the Holocaust. His intention was to purify the German Aryan race. He used the power of the government to organize the mass murder of people he considered to be impure for his race. During the twelve years that Hitler was in power, he particularly targeted Jews and Gypsies for extermination from Germany. Not only were they uprooted and placed in labor camps, but by the end of the war, five- to six million had been murdered.

Millions of other groups of people who did not fit into Hitler's plan for a supreme Aryan race were victims of the Holocaust. Political dissidents, homosexuals, Jehovah's Witnesses, the disabled, and prisoners of war were among those harassed and imprisoned in concentration camps alongside Jews and the Gypsies. These people, however, were not consistently and thoroughly targeted as groups.

Hitler's prejudice was not rooted in political or religious concerns alone. He believed the Jewish people were an evil race working to take over the world. He was not interested in converting them or expelling them from Germany. In Hitler's mind, the only adequate solution to his "Jewish problem" was complete extermination of the Jewish people.

Hitler's Holocaust policies were first aimed at defining the Jewish race and inspiring anti-Jewish, or anti-Semitic, feelings among Germans. What began as boycotts of Jewish businesses evolved into restrictions on the rights of Jews. Eventually the Nazi Party confiscated and destroyed Jewish properties and moved people into Jewish ghettos or labor camps. Life was severely restricted, and conditions were harsh. Many died of disease and malnutrition.

In 1941, the policy of the Nazi Party turned to the systematic murder of the Jewish people. As the German army advanced through Europe in the battles of World War II, it killed thousands of Jews in conquered territories. Labor camps evolved into concentration camps where people were sent to be worked to death or murdered.

The German army continued its extermination tactics until the Allied armies invaded Germany in 1945. The concentration camps that the liberating armies found in Germany shocked the world. The Holocaust took a terrible toll on the Jewish people, and the memory of it continues to haunt generations who study what happened in Germany during World War II.

United States Holocaust Memorial Museum

In 1993, a museum dedicated to the events of the Holocaust opened in **Washington, D.C.** Visitors can see photos of the individuals victimized by Nazi policies as well as evidence of personal suffering. The museum is dedicated to memorializing the tragic events of the past and educating the public in hopes of preventing the world from allowing another holocaust to happen. Since its opening, over twenty-five million people have visited the museum, and people from all over the world visit its Web site every day.

Homeland Security Department

The creation of the Office of Homeland Security, a department in the **executive branch** of the federal government, occurred less than four weeks after the **September 11, 2001, terrorist attacks**. Its charge was to protect the United States from terrorist attacks and to respond to natural disasters.

The Office of Homeland Security shares information and coordinates the activities and resources of more than twenty-two different government agencies involved in security and counterterrorism that previously had reported to many different departments. They included such departments as the Customs Service, the Secret Service (both of which had previously been part of the Treasury Department), the Federal Emergency Management Agency (FEMA; an independent agency), the U.S. **Coast Guard** (which had been part of the Transportation Department), and later the Immigration and Naturalization Service (originally part of the Justice Department).

The director of the Office of Homeland Security has the title of assistant to the president for Homeland Security, similar to the official title of the national security advisor (assistant to the president for National Security). The Homeland Security Council's members include the president, vice president, and several cabinet-level officials. In the first decade of the twenty-first century, the Office of Homeland Securities had a staff of about two hundred thousand employees. The reorganization of government agencies to create it was the biggest government restructuring in more than forty years.

In its first few years, some of the Office of Homeland Security's best known initiatives were the color-coded terrorist threat alerts, enhanced security systems in airports, and the rescue efforts after Hurricane Katrina hit the Gulf Coast and flooded large areas of **Mississippi** and **Louisiana**, including the city of New Orleans.

Homestead Act

The Homestead Act was passed in Congress on May 20, 1862. It encouraged people to move west to settle new territories by promising free land. With little money but great commitment, many families left the east to start new lives on the frontier.

The United States grew enormously in the decades before 1860. New territories expanded the country from one side of the continent to the other, and a constant stream of immigrants flowed into cities. To encourage settlement of the new lands by immigrants, Congress debated forms of the Homestead Act for years prior to its enactment.

Regional concerns prevented the Homestead Act from passing for some time. Industries of the north feared a shortage of cheap immigrant labor. Southern plantation owners resisted the competition of small farms. Those who owned small farms tended to resist the institution of

This family stands with their wagon, in Loup Valley, Nebraska, on their way to their new homestead, as part of the Homestead Act of 1862. MPI/HULTON ARCHIVE/GETTY IMAGES

slavery, and plantation owners refused to support any measure that might threaten slavery, the cheap labor of which was important to their economy. Throughout the nation, landowners were concerned about what would happen to land values in the east after cheap land became available in the west. As a result, congressional efforts to pass a homesteading measure repeatedly ended in resistance and defeat.

By 1860, so much had changed as a result of population growth that opinions were beginning to sway. There were more than enough immigrants to provide cheap labor to northern industries. Businesses began to recognize the advantages that western expansion would bring, such as new markets for industry and new access to raw materials. With such a continuous stream of new residents, the fear of dropping land values eased. Slavery issues, however, continued to dominate national politics, and Southerners still resisted any homesteading act.

The **Republican Party** platform during the election of 1860 included a push for a homesteading act. Although its candidate, **Abraham Lincoln** (1809–1865; served 1861–65), was elected, passage of such legislation was not guaranteed. The **secession** of Southern states from the Union from 1860 to 1861 and the resulting absence of their congressmen provided an opportunity to pass such a measure with little resistance.

The Homestead Act went into effect January 1, 1863. It offered 160 acres of land for the cost of a small filing fee. To qualify for the offer, a person had to be the head of a household or an individual at least twenty-one years old, a U.S. citizen or someone with plans to become a citizen, and committed to settling on the land for individual benefit. To earn the title to the land, meaning full ownership, settlers had to build a house and farm at least ten acres for five years. Alternatively, after just six months of residence, settlers could purchase the land from the government for $1.25 per acre.

From 1863 to 1880, nearly five hundred thousand applications were filed under the Homestead Act for approximately 56 million acres of land. Though the measure was meant to attract homeless immigrants throughout the east, many were too poor to be able to move west. Established American families were more often attracted to move west to earn the rights to more land.

The land often proved to be mountainous, desert, or otherwise challenging to farm. Many settlers were unable to cope with the new conditions and either sold their claims to land speculators or abandoned them. Over time, Congress passed additional measures to remedy these challenges and to continue to encourage settlement, but none of them quite lived up to expectations. By 1935, when President **Franklin D. Roosevelt** (1882–1945; served 1933–45) withdrew the remainder of the public domain from private entry, only about 285 million acres out of the original 600 million acres available had been homesteaded.

Homestead Strike

Near the end of the nineteenth century, Homestead, **Pennsylvania**, was a steel mill town with a population of more than ten thousand people. Of those inhabitants, just over thirty-four hundred were employed by Carnegie Steel Company. Of those employees, eight hundred were skilled and earned an average of $2.43 for a twelve-hour shift, or roughly twenty cents an hour. Unskilled laborers earned fourteen cents an hour.

In 1889, these wages were paid on a sliding scale that was dependent on the market price being paid for steel. This means that the higher the market price (the price paid to the steel companies by other businesses who bought their product) being paid, the higher the wages would be. If the market price dropped, so did wages. But twenty and fourteen cents an hour was the average.

This agreement between management and labor was due to expire on June 30, 1892. Of the eight hundred skilled workers, all but twenty were members of the Amalgamated Association of Iron, Steel, and Tin Workers union (formally organized association of workers that advances its members' views on wages, work hours, and labor conditions). Members were expecting better terms upon expiration of the old contract. Their expectations did not seem unrealistic. **Andrew Carnegie** (1835–1919), owner of the mill, had publicly empathized with (claimed to understand) strikers in other industries. He even implied that he understood how their frustration led to violence.

In 1892, Carnegie was out of the country visiting his homeland of Scotland. Negotiations were in the hands of Henry Clay Frick (1849–1919), chairman of Carnegie Steel. Frick was known for his hard-hearted antiunion attitude. He had no patience for workers who complained and would not tolerate rebellion in any form.

The union would not accept the new contract proposed by Carnegie Steel as it required workers to accept an 18 to 26 percent decrease in wages. Union leaders Hugh O'Donnell and John W. Gates (1855–1911) met with Frick throughout June in the hopes of reaching a compromise that both sides could accept. Frick refused to consider any negotiations. Instead, he ordered the construction of a solid-wood fence topped with barbed wire built around the mill. Workers soon called it "Fort Frick."

As meetings continued to be held without progress, frustrated workers made dummies that looked like Frick and superintendent J. A. Potter and hung them on mill property. Potter sent men to tear down the dummies, but Carnegie employees turned the water hoses on them. Frick used this event as an excuse to order a lockout (an event in which workers are forbidden to work and are refused pay). In addition to the 3 miles of fencing he had built, Frick contacted Pinkerton National Detective Agency. He paid $5 a day to each of three hundred detectives to act as guards at the mill. The detectives arrived on July 6. By this time, workers had already barricaded themselves inside the steel plant.

Frick never had the chance to carry out his plan to hire strikebreakers. Citizens of the town joined Carnegie Steel's displaced workers and confronted the Pinkerton detectives just outside the mill. With both sides armed, on July 6 they battled from 4 AM until 5 PM. It is not clear who fired the first shot, but when gunfire had ceased, seven strikers and three detectives were dead, with numerous others injured. The strikers surrendered, and on July 12 eight thousand state troopers marched into Homestead and took control.

Public opinion was initially against Carnegie Steel in this dispute—but not because of the bloodshed or the damage that resulted from the conflict. In truth, both sides were guilty of taking the law into their own hands. Instead, Americans were disturbed that a labor-management disagreement could escalate into open warfare between one of the nation's most powerful companies and one of the most highly respected labor unions. However, as details of the strike were reported to the public, sentiment turned against the labor union. Most citizens believed the workers behaved brutally and used unnecessary violence in the confrontation.

The tension between company and union worsened on July 23, when anarchist, or rebel, Alexander Berkman (1870–1936) shot and stabbed Frick in his office. Frick was not seriously injured, and Berkman was caught. But that incident put an end to the steel union. Even though Berkman was not a union member, the public was unaware of this fact and perceived his attack on Frick as merely another strategy waged by the union against management. It would be another forty years before the steel industry formed a new labor union.

Carnegie's Homestead plant reopened on July 27 with a thousand new workers under the protection of the military. The company pressed charges against O'Donnell and the strikers, but no jury would find them guilty. Both sides decided to drop the matter. The strike officially ended on November 20, 1892. Three hundred locked-out employees were re-hired and joined the newly hired workers in the mill. Under their new contract, former employees worked longer hours at a lower hourly wage than they had before the strike. Most of the strikers who were not rehired were blacklisted and found themselves unable to get jobs in the steel industry. The strike did nothing but hurt the reputation of labor unions throughout the country.

Although Carnegie privately wrote letters to Frick in support of Frick's handling of the affair, Carnegie publicly implied that Frick was responsible for the tragic events stemming from the strike and asked him to resign as chairman. In spite of his departure from the steel firm, Frick was rewarded handsomely when Carnegie bought Frick's stocks in the company for $15 million.

Herbert Hoover

Herbert Hoover was inaugurated as the thirty-first president of the United States in March 1929. Despite the economic prosperity that existed then, the country would be mired in the worst financial crisis of its history soon after Hoover took office. Though Hoover involved the federal government in fixing the country's economic problems more than preceding presidents had done, his efforts were deemed "too little, too late" by many Americans.

Herbert Hoover was inaugurated as the thirty-first president of the United States in March 1929. The country would be hindered by the worst financial crisis of its history soon after Hoover took office. THE LIBRARY OF CONGRESS

Early life

Herbert Clark Hoover was born August 10, 1874, in West Branch, **Iowa**, a small Quaker settlement near Iowa City. His father, Jesse Hoover, was a village blacksmith and merchant. Hulda Randall Minthorn Hoover, his mother, was an active lay minister in the Society of Friends, which the **Quakers** had come to be called. Both died when Hoover was quite young, his father in 1880, then his mother in 1884.

Hoover and his two siblings were separated and sent to live with other family members. Hoover was sent to live with his uncle, Henry John Minthorn, in Newberg, **Oregon**. Though he attended school at first, Hoover soon dropped out to oversee the daily operations of his uncle's real estate business.

Hoover attended night school to develop his business and office skills. Living with his oppressive uncle left Hoover with an independent spirit and a determination to earn his own financial freedom. So Hoover left Oregon to attend Stanford University in **California** in 1891.

Herbert Hoover took advantage of the innovative curriculum at Stanford. He received an excellent education in geology and participated in college politics. It was at Stanford that Hoover met the woman he would later marry, Lou Henry, a fellow geology student.

After graduation in 1895, Hoover worked as a day laborer in the Reward Gold Mine in Grass City, California. In 1896, he got an office job at an important mining firm in San Francisco, California. His experience and promotions there eventually led in 1897 to a position with one of the world's leading mining consulting firms, Bewick, Moreing, and Company of London, England.

The company sent Hoover to Australia, where he proved his worth as a mining engineer by recommending several successful mine purchases for the company. He was quickly considered a success and an authority in his field, making a staggering salary of $10,000 per year. He soon proposed marriage to Lou Henry, and they were married in 1899.

In 1898, Hoover went to China on behalf of Bewick, Moreing, to exploit extensive and profitable coal deposits. While he was there, Chinese nationalists rebelling against foreign powers began the Boxer Rebellion. In exchange for helping the Chinese government defend against the rebellion, Hoover was given control of the Chinese Engineering and Mining Company. He used the company to buy a share of partnership in Bewick, Moreing. Hoover's later business deals in places such as Sri Lanka, Russia, Egypt, Zimbabwe, Burma, and Malaysia helped him to amass a great fortune.

In 1901, the Hoovers moved to London, where they had two children. Hoover was drawn to move beyond amassing great fortunes and started to consider philanthropic ways to apply his skills. When **World War I** (1914–18) broke out in 1914, he found his opportunity.

A new career

When war started in August 1914, the American ambassador to Britain asked for Hoover's assistance to aid Americans stranded abroad at the onset of war. Hoover did this with such efficiency that he was asked to oversee the Commission for Relief in Belgium (CRB) to help people in German-occupied Belgium. The CRB operated much like a state, with

4,000 committees worldwide, 130,000 volunteers, and $200 million in gifts and subsidies. Hoover's extraordinary diplomatic skill, his knowledge of worldwide shipping, and his determination and perseverance kept a steady flow of food to Belgium.

In May 1917, U.S. president **Woodrow Wilson** (1856–1924; served 1913–21) appointed Hoover food administrator for the United States during its involvement in World War I. In that role, Hoover stimulated agricultural production, controlled surging farm prices, and was able to ship food surpluses to a famished Europe.

Hoover took part in the Paris Peace Conference of 1919 to negotiate peace treaties after World War I. He held a variety of positions: chairman of the Inter-Allied Food Council, director general of the American Relief Administration, economic director of the Supreme Economic Council, chairman of the European Coal Council, and personal advisor to President Wilson.

Secretary of commerce

By 1920, rumblings about nominating Hoover for the presidency were heard among both Republicans and Democrats. Though a Hoover nomination did not happen that year, his backing of Republican **Warren G. Harding** (1865–1923; served 1921–23), who became the next president, earned Hoover a new position as the secretary of commerce, the head of the U.S. Department of Commerce.

Hoover was secretary of commerce from 1921 to 1929 under both President Harding and President **Calvin Coolidge** (1872–1933; served 1923–29). In this role, Hoover encouraged the formation of trade associations, pushed cooperative markets for farmers, and was particularly aggressive in seeking overseas markets for American businesses. His greatest aim was for commercial expansion to replace military investment for bringing peace and prosperity to the world.

In 1927, the Mississippi River flooded, which left 350,000 people destitute. Dominating the headlines, Hoover directed the feeding, clothing, and housing of the stricken families. Such publicity made him the most famous secretary of commerce in U.S. history, and in 1928 Hoover was nominated and elected president of the United States.

An advertisement for a Herbert Hoover campaign film promoting his bid for presidency, circa 1928. © CORBIS

Presidency

When Herbert Hoover was inaugurated in March 1929, the United States was enjoying a period of prosperity. U.S. business was growing, manufactured goods and raw materials flowed from the United States to the rest of the world, and technology was developing at an impressive rate. The prosperity, however, was far from evenly distributed, and there were many who were doing poorly, too.

In time, manufacturers started to have too much inventory and began to allow installment payments, or credit, for purchases. Those who had a little to invest risked their earnings in the stock market, which is the market for buying and selling shares in large companies. Often people bought stocks on margin, which meant they only paid a fraction of the total cost for the stock and borrowed the rest. If stock prices went up, investors repaid the borrowed amount and pocketed the profit. However, if stocks went down, investors lost the entire investment if they could not repay the borrowed money to the broker.

On October 24, 1929, stock prices plummeted. Prices continued to dive as investors scrambled to sell their stocks, and thousands of people lost their savings. It marked the beginning of the **Great Depression** (1929–41; a time of economic downturn in the United States) and Hoover's greatest challenge.

Domestic recovery

In November 1929, Hoover gathered railroad, labor, and construction leaders along with mayors and governors. In December, he gathered groups of business, labor, and farm leaders, too. Warning of a serious recession, Hoover worked to place the responsibility for avoiding major catastrophe within their hands. He asked them to foster industrial expansion, avoid strikes, share work when possible, stabilize prices, and provide relief where needed. Most of all, he stressed that there must not be drastic wage cuts. He pushed both national and state public offices to employ people out of work, asking Congress and state governors to appropriate, or provide the funds needed, for such jobs.

Though it seemed that Hoover's policies were working by spring 1930, by fall economic conditions had again worsened. Employers were forced to cut production. Hoover responded by creating the President's Emergency Committee for Unemployment, which established three thousand local committees. By June 1931, $2 billion was being spent and a million men were being employed on federal projects. Despite occasional rallies in the economic indicators, by 1932 over 20 percent of the labor force was unemployed, and only one-quarter of the unemployed was receiving relief assistance.

The most important effort Hoover made to bring relief was the recovery program called the Reconstruction Finance Corporation (RFC). The RFC started in January 1932. That year it provided loans to over five thousand banks, railroads, life insurance companies, farm mortgage associations, and building and loan associations. It saved many businesses from failure, halting further financial collapse and restoring some public confidence.

Though Hoover took great steps to bring relief to the country, he had two personal limits that reduced his popularity with the public and contributed to his inability to win another term as president. He opposed offering direct federal aid to the unemployed. Believing such aid would lower wages to a bare minimum and reward laziness, he insisted that unemployment relief was a problem for local governments. Hoover also was against any policies that might shift the budget out of balance by spending more federal money than the government was collecting in taxes and other revenues. In Hoover's opinion, a balanced federal budget was the keystone of recovery.

The Bonus Army March

By spring 1932, there were signs of social unease and community disruptions. Hunger marches took place, and the unemployed rioted. The most memorable event was the gathering of World War I veterans in **Washington, D.C.** Known as the Bonus Army, the eleven thousand veterans marched in front of the White House and the Capitol demanding an early payment of a bonus not scheduled for distribution until 1945. They camped in abandoned buildings and in tents at Anacostia Flats, across the river from the Capitol, waiting for Congress to make a decision.

When payment was rejected by Congress, most men returned home. A minority, however, refused to leave the buildings, and Hoover instructed that the men be evicted. Both his secretary of war, Patrick Hurley (1883–1963), and U.S. Army general **Douglas MacArthur** (1880–1964) took disastrous steps to carry out the eviction. The veterans were pushed back far beyond their camps with the use of tanks, guns, and tear gas. Two veterans were killed. Hoover was personally horrified, but instead of blaming Hurley and MacArthur, he took personal responsibility and suffered the resulting negative opinions.

Foreign policies

The economic problems of the Great Depression affected the rest of the developed world, and President Hoover's challenges extended beyond the nation's borders, too. He met those challenges with the intention of maintaining peace. To ease the global depression, he allowed nations to delay payment of debts to the United States for a year.

In Asia, Japan was launching military attacks against China. The Hoover administration's Stimson Doctrine stated that the United States would not recognize any unilateral change in Asia imposed by force. The United States, however, refrained from supporting China with military intervention.

Hoover promoted international disarmament, or the voluntary reduction in arms worldwide. He also initiated the "good neighbor" policy, which implied the United States would refrain from intervening in other country's politics.

Post-presidential years

President Hoover only served one term as president, losing to **Franklin D. Roosevelt** in the 1932 election, but he continued to be vocal and active after his presidency. During **World War II** (1939–45) Hoover launched relief efforts in German-occupied Poland and Finland.

In 1946, President **Harry S. Truman** (1884–1972; served 1945–53) appointed Hoover honorary chairman of the Famine Emergency Committee. In 1947, Truman named Hoover to head the Committee on Organization of the Executive Branch of Government, now known as the Hoover Commission. Hoover's job was to evaluate the structure and operation of the **executive branch** of government and to recommend improvements. He performed this service again for President **Dwight D. Eisenhower** (1890–1969; served 1953–61) in 1953.

Until the end of his life, Hoover wrote a number of books, including three memoirs and several volumes on his relief activities. He also wrote multiple defenses of his governmental policies. Herbert Hoover died in New York City on October 20, 1964.

J. Edgar Hoover

J. Edgar Hoover served in the **Federal Bureau of Investigation** (FBI) for over fifty years, mostly at the head of the organization as its director. Hoover built the FBI from a small organization with a poor reputation into a powerful, secretive, and controversial law enforcement bureau.

Early life

Hoover was born on January 1, 1895, in **Washington, D.C.** Raised in a family of Scottish Presbyterians, Hoover spent his life believing that middle-class Protestant morality was the core of American society and values. His mother, Anna Marie Scheitlin, was strict and religious. His father, Dickerson Hoover, was a civil servant who suffered from poor health.

Hoover excelled in school as a child, eventually attending Central High School, an all-white school from which he graduated at the top of his class in 1913. During his youth, he also worked to help his family, including delivering groceries for neighbors. Hoover received a full scholarship to attend the University of Virginia, but his family could not afford housing there. Hoover instead worked in the day and studied law at night at George Washington University in the District of Columbia. He received a bachelor's degree in 1916 and a master's degree in 1917.

Early career

During **World War I** (1914–18) Hoover got a job in the U.S. Department of Justice. He began in the mail room but soon was transferred to the Emergency War Division of the Alien Enemy section. There Hoover administered the federal regulations that applied to German and Austro-Hungarian aliens (those who held citizenship in the land of their birth but lived in the United States) being supervised by the federal government during the war.

In autumn 1918, the Bolshevik Revolution began in Russia. Strikes in Vancouver, British Columbia, and Seattle, **Washington**, raised fears of a similar communist revolt in either Canada or the United States. Early the next year, Hoover became a special assistant to U.S. attorney general A. Mitchell Palmer (1872–1936), whose home was bombed that spring. In the ensuing years, Palmer ordered and Hoover supervised a series of "red raids" for arresting and deporting aliens who were members of communist organizations. In this work, Hoover spied on lawyers representing alien suspects.

The Bureau of Investigation

When a new attorney general became head of the Justice Department in 1921, Hoover became the assistant director of the Bureau of Investigation (BI). At the time, the BI had very little law enforcement authority under federal law. It was filled with employees who got their jobs through political favoritism. It was in this environment that Hoover was elevated to director of the BI in 1924, the position he would keep until his death in 1972. Hoover accepted the job on the conditions that he have full control over hiring and that he report directly to the attorney general rather than to a lower-level official in the Department of Justice.

Hoover worked hard to convert the BI into a respected law enforcement bureau. He fired incapable employees and hired young agents with backgrounds in law and accountancy. He created a crime laboratory and organized a fingerprint division for collecting fingerprints from across the nation into a central location. He opened a national academy for training BI agents. He also created a highly organized filing system for handling the BI's public and secret files. In 1935, the bureau was renamed the Federal Bureau of Investigation (FBI).

Hoover never married. Prior to joining the bureau he had romanced a woman who chose an army officer over Hoover. Hoover lived with his mother until her death and then lived alone the rest of his life. Outside of work, he enjoyed attending baseball games and horse races and collecting Asian art.

From gangsters to activists

In the 1930s, the FBI earned a reputation for fighting gangsters such as Pretty Boy Floyd (1901–1934), Machine Gun Kelly (1895–1954), and John Dillinger (1903–1934). In the 1940s, Hoover began to report directly to President **Franklin D. Roosevelt** (1882–1945; served 1933–45). At Roosevelt's direction, Hoover built the FBI's domestic surveillance system. The system was useful for investigating the domestic activities of communists, whom the federal government targeted during another "red scare" of the 1950s.

During the late 1950s, Hoover and the FBI developed a counterintelligence program called COINTELPRO. Under the program, the FBI spied on American citizens, often breaking laws against wiretapping and microphone surveillance. Hoover used COINTELRO to investigate communists, the **Ku Klux Klan**, black activist organizations such as the **Black Panther Party**, and civil rights activists, including **Martin Luther King Jr.** (1929–1968). Hoover viewed civil rights activists as part of the communist threat to America.

In the 1960s, President **John F. Kennedy** (1917–1963; served 1961–63) required Hoover to report to Attorney General **Robert F. Kennedy** (1925–1968) rather than directly to the president. Hoover and the Kennedys did not get along well.

End of life

Hoover died on May 2, 1972. During his life, he generally had a positive reputation with Americans, though political and civil rights activists were concerned with his goals and methods. After enactment of the **Freedom of Information Act**, Americans were able to view FBI records that revealed some of the extent to which Hoover violated federal law to investigate Americans. These revelations tarnished Hoover's reputation in the eyes of many. Other Americans, however, believe enforcement of federal criminal laws is more important than protecting the civil rights of citizens. This debate survives today under the question of the federal government's power to fight what it calls the war on terrorism.

Hoovervilles

In October 1929, the United States stock market crashed. It signaled the beginning of a major economic crisis that would last for years and extend beyond the nation to affect the rest of the world. Throughout this time, called the **Great Depression** (1929–41), many people lost their savings, their jobs, and their homes.

When President **Herbert Hoover** (1874–1964; served 1929–33) took office the March before the crash, it seemed that the United States was enjoying a period of general prosperity. The economy was thriving. U.S. business was growing, manufactured goods and raw materials flowed from the United States to the rest of the world, and technology was developing at an impressive rate.

The economy, however, was not as strong as it appeared, and many things led to its collapse. Because most citizens were unaware of these factors, they blamed the new president for the onset of the Great Depression. Though Hoover worked to alleviate the nation's economic hardships, he was also against providing direct assistance to the unemployed. He believed such assistance would lower wages to a bare minimum and reward laziness. As a result, some Americans began to use his name to describe the miserable conditions in which they lived.

By 1931, thousands of people had become unemployed and homeless. Shantytowns began to appear throughout the country, mostly within the inner cities, where people built makeshift homes. They built their homes out of cardboard, tin, crates, scrap lumber, and other discarded materials. These communities were quickly dubbed "Hoovervilles."

The residents of Hoovervilles often assembled simple governments of their own, electing a mayor, city council, and police chief. Tenement houses were bought and sold like other homes, though prices rarely exceeded $30. City health, fire, and law enforcement officials closely regulated many Hoovervilles. They often enacted requirements that tenements be above ground, have a certain number of windows, and be kept clear of debris and human waste.

People also used Hoover's name to label other aspects of the experiences of the poor. When a jobless man wrapped a newspaper around him for warmth, the paper was called a Hoover blanket. When a broken-down automobile was being towed away by mules, it was a Hoover wagon. A man would turn an empty pocket inside out and call it a Hoover flag. Jackrabbits were called Hoover hogs by people who could not afford pork products.

The nation did not begin to recover from the Great Depression until the mid-1930s under the **New Deal** programs of President **Franklin D. Roosevelt** (1882–1945; served 1933–45). Full recovery came after the United States entered **World War II** in 1941. The war improved jobs and wages by creating a high demand for manufactured products. Most Hoovervilles disappeared by the onset of war in 1941, though a number lingered through the early 1950s.

House of Burgesses

Virginia's House of Burgesses was the first representative assembly in North America. It was created by Governor George Yeardley (c. 1587–1627) under instructions from the Virginia Company of London, which owned the colony of Virginia. In hope of attracting more immigrants to its colony, the company replaced a form of martial law used by the colony's previous governor with English common law.

The new system provided for local governments as well as a general assembly for the whole colony. Virginia was organized at first into cities, or boroughs. Monthly courts were created in 1622. Further legislation created shires in 1634 and counties in 1642. The general assembly was called the House of Burgesses. It contained representatives from each of the local boroughs.

The House of Burgesses borrowed its name from the House of Commons in England, whose representatives were called burgesses. It

Virginia's House of Burgesses was the first representative assembly in North America. The new system provided for local governments as well as a general assembly for the whole colony. MPI/HULTON ARCHIVE/GETTY IMAGES

functioned as a simple parliament that passed legislation for the entire colony of Virginia. The Virginia Company appointed a governor and a council as part of the legislature. The other members were elected, two by each of Virginia's ten settlements.

The first elected assembly gathered in the House of Burgesses on July 30, 1619, in Jamestown. It met for five days. There were twenty-two members present. The House of Burgesses continued to meet annually, even after the dissolution of the Virginia Company in 1624 brought the colony under direct royal control.

House of Representatives

See **Checks and Balances; Legislative Branch**

House Un-American Activities Committee

In 1938, the U.S. House of Representatives established the House Un-American Activities Committee (HUAC). With communist and fascist regimes posing threats to the security of European countries, Congress decided to investigate the potential of danger in the United States. HUAC had the responsibility of investigating un-American propaganda and activities that might threaten national security. It focused mostly on communist and fascist organizations. Its guidelines, however, were vague enough that many people who simply disagreed with government policy found themselves under scrutiny by the committee.

Defining a purpose

Because HUAC was led by U.S. representative Martin Dies Jr. (1900–1972) of **Texas**, it was also called the Dies Committee. It was not the first committee of its kind to be established by Congress. Earlier committees did similar work in 1919, 1930, and 1934. HUAC's broadly aimed and aggressive activities, however, made it controversial and memorable.

Sponsors of the motion to establish HUAC expected it to reduce the potential threat of foreign agents and subversive activities by communist and fascist interests. Under the leadership of Dies, however, the term "un-American" gained a broader definition, and many without communist or fascist ties were investigated. HUAC investigations became a means to suppress any dissent, often with the effect of undermining the freedoms of speech, press, and assembly. Liberals, intellectuals, artists, labor leaders, immigrants, Jews, and African Americans found themselves targets of HUAC investigations.

After **World War II** (1939–45) HUAC became a permanent committee. The global environment of the **Cold War** (1945–91) after World War II allowed the committee to be particularly aggressive and manipulative in its tactics. Fear of communists, foreigners, and independent thinkers made the American public tolerant of HUAC's actions. As a result, many people were harassed, and some found their lives irrevocably changed as a result.

The Hollywood Ten

The HUAC investigations of members of Hollywood were viewed by many as a witch hunt. More than one hundred witnesses from the industry were called before HUAC during its existence. Eight screenwriters and two directors famously refused to answer the questions asked of them. Known as the Hollywood Ten, they depended on their **Fifth Amendment** right to be free from self-incrimination and their **First Amendment** right to freedom of speech and assembly.

In reaction, HUAC charged the Hollywood Ten with contempt of Congress. An investigative grand jury upheld the accusations and found the witnesses guilty as charged. The Hollywood Ten lost an appeal to an appellate court, and a conservative **Supreme Court** refused to hear the case. As a result, the Ten were forced to serve up to a year in a federal prison. These events initiated the studios' practice of firing and blacklisting artists with suspected communist connections.

Hollywood and beyond

One of the most famous aspects of the HUAC investigations involved Hollywood. In 1947, the committee devoted nine days to questioning members of the **movie** industry. Producers, actors, directors, and writers were questioned. In all, forty-one witnesses were called. They included leading figures and famous actors like Walt Disney (1901–1966), Gary Cooper (1901–1961), and future U.S. president **Ronald Reagan** (1911–2004; served 1981–89).

Nineteen Hollywood witnesses were classified as unfriendly prior to appearing before the committee. Each witness faced the question of whether they or others they knew were ever involved with the Communist Party. Although HUAC was challenging their industry, Hollywood studios chose to support it publicly. As a result of the investigations, they fired artists with suspected or proven communist connections. These names were accumulated on an unofficial but highly damaging blacklist. Those who were blacklisted could not find work anywhere in the industry. More than three hundred people were blacklisted, and only a small number ever managed to recover their careers. (See **Hollywood Blacklisting**.)

Among those called from Hollywood, ten witnesses refused to testify. They were charged with contempt of Congress and sent to prison. With the support of the court system behind them, the committee was encouraged to act even more aggressively. By the 1950s, HUAC was investigating subversives in government, labor **unions**, the press, and religious organizations as well as Hollywood. Fearing the committee's unchecked power, many witnesses falsely accused others. With little chance to establish their innocence, many people had their lives forever altered by a HUAC summons. With public suspicions aroused, people lost their jobs and their friends.

Decline

HUAC began to decline in popularity throughout the 1950s. Similar investigations in the Senate under a committee led by U.S. senator **Joseph McCarthy** (1908–1957) of **Wisconsin** began to divert attention from HUAC activities. Growing liberalism in the late 1950s and 1960s encouraged public intolerance for such investigations. By the 1960s, HUAC was losing influence and was less active. HUAC was officially abolished in January 1975.

Sam Houston

Sam Houston was the first president of the Independent Republic of **Texas**, and he later served as governor of the state of Texas.

Houston was born on March 2, 1793, and had little, if any, formal schooling. His family moved from **Virginia** to **Tennessee** in 1806, and there Houston grew to adulthood. He served in the **War of 1812** (1812–15) as a lieutenant in the U.S. **Army**, commanded by General **Andrew Jackson** (1767–1845). After the war, Houston returned to Tennessee, studied law, and became an attorney.

Joins the Cherokees

Houston was elected to the U.S. Congress in 1823. Four years later, he became governor of Tennessee. In 1829, he married Eliza H. Allen, but the marriage soon came to a sudden end. Divorce was highly uncommon at the time, and the public was scandalized. Houston never told anyone what had gone wrong, but considering himself a ruined man, he resigned the governorship. He moved to **Indian Territory** west of the Mississippi River to start a new life among a band of Cherokees that he had known since childhood.

In Indian Territory, Houston took a Native American name, wore Indian dress, became a tribal citizen, and married a Cherokee woman. He lived among the Cherokees until 1832, when he left his Indian wife and migrated to Texas. At that time, Texas was a Mexican province in political turmoil because of the increasing number of Anglo-Americans moving into the area.

Texas revolutionary

Houston took an active role with those in Texas who wanted more self-rule and less interference from Mexico City. He signed the Texas Declaration of Independence and was selected commanding general of the Texan army on March 4, 1836.

Soon, bands of Texans, disobeying Houston's orders, captured Mexican forts at the **Alamo** and Goliad. By the end of March 1836, both forts had been recaptured by Mexican troops and their Texan defenders wiped out. Nearly two hundred Americans were killed at the Alamo.

After the defeat at the Alamo, Houston turned his small army eastward and rapidly fled toward the **Louisiana** border in a retreat popularly known as the "Runaway Scrape." The Mexican army, led by General Antonio López de Santa Anna (1794–1876), pursued Houston's army. On April 21, 1836, Houston surprised the Mexican general by suddenly turning his troops and attacking the Mexican army. In the ensuing battle, known as the Battle of San Jacinto, nearly half the Mexicans died and the rest, including General Santa Anna, were taken prisoner. The Texans lost only six men.

President of Texas

Houston's spectacular victory in the Battle of San Jacinto ended the war and assured Texan independence. It also led to Houston's election as president of the Independent Republic of Texas in the summer of 1836. As president, Houston's main goal was to arrange for the United States to annex, or add, Texas to the Union as quickly as possible. American politics in the years leading to the American **Civil War** (1861–65) were divided, and delayed Texas's entry into the Union.

Texas finally became a state in 1845, and Houston was elected to represent the state in the U.S. Senate. Although Texas was firmly a part of the South, Houston rejected many of the Southern political causes of the 1850s. He believed in preserving the Union over Southern sectionalism (favoring one's region over one's country). In 1859, he became governor of Texas, and in early 1861 he refused to cooperate with the state's **secession** convention, the formal meeting at which Texas decided to withdraw from the Union. He also declined to take an oath of allegiance to the newly formed **Confederate States of America**.

Soon Houston was forced to retire from the governorship because of his Unionist views. His ejection from the governor's office embittered him and soured his few remaining years.

HUAC
See **House Un-American Activities Committee**

Edwin Hubble

Edwin Hubble made two major contributions to American science. At a time when it was believed that the universe ended with the Milky Way, Hubble proved the existence of other galaxies, and he showed that the universe was expanding. He developed a mathematical concept to quantify this expansion, known as Hubble's law.

Edwin Powell Hubble was born on November 20, 1889, the third of seven children. The family lived in **Missouri** until 1898, when they relocated to Chicago, **Illinois**. Hubble excelled in both academics and sports, graduating from high school in 1906 at the age of sixteen. An academic scholarship sent him to the University of Chicago, where he graduated with a bachelor's degree in mathematics and astronomy in 1910.

In 1910, Hubble traveled to England to study at Oxford University as a Rhodes Scholar. In addition to his law studies there, he continued to pursue his athletic interests. Hubble returned to the United States in 1913 and began practicing law. Boredom set in within the first year, and he returned to the University of Chicago to work toward a Ph.D. in astronomy.

Mount Wilson

Hubble began working under the supervision of the school's Yerkes Observatory director. During this time, he met astronomer George E. Hale (1868–1938), the founder of the Yerkes Observatory and director of the Mount Wilson Observatory in **California**. The director invited Hubble to join the Mount Wilson staff once he received his degree, and Hubble accepted the offer. After serving in the army in **World War I** (1914–18) and being discharged in 1917, Hubble began his work at Mount Wilson. He stayed at the institution throughout his career.

In 1923, Hubble observed galaxies outside the Milky Way. His discovery of the existence of other galaxies—he would eventually discover nine—was announced publicly in 1924. That same year, he married Grace Burke Leib. The following year, Hubble introduced a system for classifying these galaxies, which became the basis for the modern classification system used by astronomers.

Determining distance using Hubble's law

Hubble continued to study galaxies throughout the 1920s. During this time, he measured the distances of more than twenty galaxies. But 1929 would prove to be the year of Hubble's most important discovery.

For over a decade, scientists predicted that the light coming from distant galaxies might indicate that they were moving apart from each other and away from Earth. If they were speeding fast enough away from Earth, that motion would stretch the light waves emitting from them. This stretching was called the redshift because longer wavelengths make light take on a reddish hue.

Hubble's most famous achievement was to determine the redshifts for a large number of galaxies by measuring the wavelengths of light emitting from them. His measurements told him that distant galaxies did move away from Earth. He also learned that the farther away these galaxies were from Earth, the faster they moved. The relationship between a galaxy's distance and its speed eventually became known as Hubble's law.

Big bang theory

Hubble's observations gave scientists a place to start when trying to determine the age of the universe and how it began. Some experts, such as British astronomer Fred Hoyle (1915–2001), theorized that the universe existed in a steady state, without beginning or end. Others raised the possibility that the origin of the universe was a single point from which everything else—space, time, and matter—had expanded. Astronomers proposed that this expansion had begun with a huge explosion, called the Big Bang, a phrase coined by Hoyle.

Hubble refused to get involved in the argument. Instead, he viewed his role as one of observing and reporting. Instead of saying galaxies were moving, he claimed they *appeared* to be moving.

Mount Palomar

Hubble had become America's leading astronomer by the 1930s. He was in charge of the Mount Wilson Observatory and mentored an entire generation of younger astronomers who studied there. His work extended beyond Mount Wilson, however, and he was intimately involved in the planning and construction of a new 200-inch telescope at Mount Palomar observatory in southern California. The telescope was named the Hale, after Hubble's own mentor.

Hubble headed an army research department during **World War II** (1939–45). He had the honor of being the first to use the Hale telescope when it was completed in 1948. The esteemed astronomer continued to work at Mount Wilson and Mount Palomar until his death on September 28, 1953, of a stroke.

Henry Hudson

Henry Hudson was an English navigator and explorer. North America has a bay, a strait, and a river named for him. In his short life, he sailed at least three times for English companies and at least once for a Dutch company. His goal, which eluded him, was to find a navigable passage from Europe to Asia through the Arctic region. Instead, he made discoveries that eventually opened European trading with the natives in North America.

Very little is known about Hudson's birth and early life. The earliest record from his life concerns a voyage he took in 1607. The Muscovy Company of England hired him to search for a navigable passage around the north coast of Siberia to China. He was unable to find the so-called Northeast Passage, either on that voyage or on another he took in 1608.

Dutch East India Company

In 1609, the **Dutch East India Company** hired Hudson to search for the Northeast Passage aboard the ship called *Half Moon*. The Dutch East India Company was a company from Netherlands and one of the first modern corporations. It financed voyages to the East Indies (present day Indonesia) to make money trading European goods for Asian spices and other goods.

The *Half Moon* hit heavy ice off the northern coast of Norway. Hudson's crew refused to go further, but Hudson did not want to return to the Netherlands. A fellow explorer, **John Smith** (c. 1580–1631), who colonized **Virginia**, had corresponded with Hudson, passing along maps concerning the New World. Hudson turned the ship around and headed west to look for a Northwest Passage to Asia.

Sailed through New York's harbor

The voyagers reached the coast of Nova Scotia in July 1609, then sailed down to the Chesapeake Bay and up to Delaware Bay. In September, they reached the entrance to what would be called New York Harbor. Italian explorer Giovanni da Verrazano (c. 1485–c. 1528) had been there in 1524, but Hudson was the first European to sail through the harbor up the river that would eventually bear his name. By coincidence, French explorer **Samuel de Champlain** (c. 1567–1635) was in the region of Lake Champlain around this time.

The *Half Moon* made it as far as present-day Albany, **New York**. Hudson's crew had occasional problems with Native Americans and also learned that the area was rich with natural resources, including animals with valuable furs. Heading back down the river, Hudson and company stayed in New York Harbor for a few days at a place that Hudson wrote was called "Manna-hata" by the natives. It would eventually be called Manhattan in New York City.

Caught between British and Dutch interests

Hudson's discovery of valuable resources in the New World encouraged investors in the Netherlands to form the **Dutch West India Company**. English authorities, however, told Hudson not to sail anymore for Dutch companies. Hudson found English investors to finance another search for the Northwest Passage.

Hudson left for North America in April 1610 aboard the ship *Discovery*. He planned to sail north of where his last voyage had gone. By June, he sighted Resolution Island, which separates Davis Strait from Hudson Strait in northeastern Canada. The *Discovery* took six weeks to navigate the Hudson Strait before reaching the large Canadian bay that would be called Hudson Bay. Hudson thought he had reached the Pacific Ocean.

The *Discovery* turned south, eventually entering James Bay, where Hudson and his crew learned that they were landlocked. They had not found the Northwest Passage. Unprepared for this October setback and with the bay freezing in November, they had to spend the winter in the region with few supplies.

Left to die

In June 1611, the ice had melted enough for the *Discovery* to sail for home. When the ship reached Charlton Island in the southern part of James Bay, the crew mutinied. A leader of the mutiny, Robert Juet, had sailed with Hudson on his previous voyage. The mutineers stranded Hudson, his nineteen-year-old son John, and some weaker crewmembers in a small vessel on the bay. Historians presume that Hudson and his stranded companions died in the region that year. History has no record of Hudson afterward.

Dolores Huerta

[Dolores Huerta is cofounder and first vice president of the **United Farm Workers** union. She has dedicated much of her life to the struggle for justice and dignity for migrant farm workers.

Dolores Fernández Huerta was born in a small mining town in northern **New Mexico** in 1930. When Huerta was a toddler, her parents divorced, and she moved to **California** with her mother and two brothers. By this point, the severe economic slowdown known as the **Great Depression** (1929–41) was fully underway, making it hard for many Americans to earn a living. Her mother worked at a cannery at night and as a waitress during the day, while Huerta's grandfather helped watch the children. By the 1940s, the family's financial situation improved. Huerta's mother, who had remarried, owned a restaurant and hotel, and Huerta and her brothers helped run both businesses.

Labor leader and civil rights activist Dolores Huerta was cofounder and first vice president of the United Farm Workers union. AP IMAGES

Inspired by father's accomplishments

Huerta was separated from her father, but the two remained in contact. His work activities inspired her. He had become active in labor **unions** and eventually returned to school to earn a college degree. In 1938, he won election to the New Mexico state legislature where he worked to enact better labor laws.

After high school, Huerta went to college and earned a teaching certificate, but she soon realized she wanted to do more than teach children. She wanted to help those who came to school barefoot and hungry.

Turns to social activism

In the mid-1950s, Huerta began to work for the Community Service Organization (CSO), a Mexican American self-help association founded in Los Angeles. She registered people to vote, organized citizenship classes for immigrants, and pressed local governments for improvements in barrios (Spanish-speaking neighborhoods). As a result of her skills, the CSO sent her to Sacramento, California, to work as a lobbyist (a person who persuades legislators to vote for certain laws).

During the late 1950s, Huerta became concerned about the living and working conditions of farm workers. Life for migrant farm workers was incredibly harsh. They worked in the hot sun for hours, picking crops. They often slept in run-down shacks or in their cars. Farm owners paid the workers poor wages and often tricked them out of the meager wages they had earned.

Chávez and the UFW

Huerta joined the Agricultural Workers Association, a community interest group in northern California. Through the AWA, she met **César Chávez** (1927–1993), the director of the CSO in California and **Arizona**. Chávez shared her deep interest in farm workers. Unhappy with the CSO's unwillingness to form a union for farm workers, Chávez and Huerta left to found the National Farm Workers Association in Delano, California, in 1962. After 1972, the union would be known simply as the United Farm Workers (UFW).

As second-in-command to Chávez, Huerta helped shape and guide the union. In 1965, when Delano grape workers went on strike, she devised the strategy for the strike and led the workers on the picket lines. Afterward, she became the union's first contract negotiator. In the late 1960s, she directed the grape boycott on the East Coast. Her work there helped bring about a successful grape boycott across the nation.

Huerta's style was forceful and uncompromising. However, she succeeded in bringing together feminists, community workers, religious groups, Hispanic associations, student protesters, and peace groups to fight for the rights of migrant farm workers. Victory finally came in 1975 when California governor Jerry Brown (1938–) signed the Agricultural Labor Relations Act, the first bill of rights for farm workers ever enacted in America. It allowed them to form a union that would negotiate with farm owners for better wages and working conditions.

UFW activities

Over the years, Huerta has committed her energies to the UFW as a leader, speaker, fund-raiser, negotiator, picket captain, and adviser to government leaders. In the 1980s, she helped found the union's radio station in California. She testified before state and federal committees on a range of issues, including the use of pesticides on crops and other health matters facing migrant workers.

Many of Huerta's activities on behalf of the UFW have placed her in personal danger. She was arrested more than twenty times. In 1988, during a peaceful protest demonstration in San Francisco, Huerta was severely injured by baton-swinging police officers. She suffered two broken ribs and a ruptured spleen, forcing her to undergo emergency surgery. The incident outraged the public and caused the San Francisco police department to change its rules regarding crowd control and discipline.

Legacy of the UFW

After recovering from her life-threatening injuries, Huerta resumed her work on behalf of farm workers and in other political areas. In 2006, Princeton University gave her an honorary degree. Huerta is the mother of eleven children.

Human Genome Project

In 1990, the U.S. Department of Energy and the National Institutes of Health initiated a project to map the human genome. They hoped that, through enormous effort, scientists could locate and identify the tens of thousands of genes that make up the human body and find out what each one of them actually does. The multibillion dollar Human Genome Project (HGP) was expected to take fifteen years to complete.

The actual work of mapping the human genome was done at hundreds of laboratories and university research units throughout the nation and was funded by the government. The United States coordinated its work with related programs in several other countries, and thus the Human Genome Project became an international undertaking involving at least eighteen countries. It was by far the largest coordinated effort ever undertaken in the biological sciences.

Basic terminology

The "human genome" is the term used to describe the complete collection of genes found in a single set of human chromosomes. It is contained inside the nucleus of each one of the human body's several trillion cells and provides all the information necessary for the body to live and grow. It is, in essence, a master blueprint for building a man or woman.

DNA (deoxyribonucleic acid) is the genetic material that contains the code for all living things. A DNA molecule consists of two long chains or strands joined together by chemicals called bases or nucleotides, all of which are coiled together into a twisted-ladder shape called a double helix. The bases are considered to be the "rungs" of the twisted ladder. These rungs are made up of only four different types of nucleotides—adenine (A), thymine (T), guanine (G), and cytosine (C). The four bases always form a "rung" in pairs, and they always pair up in the same way: A always pairs with T, and G always pairs with C. What is most important about these pairs of bases is the particular order of the As, Ts, Gs, and Cs. Their order dictates whether an organism is a human being, a bumblebee, or an apple.

Each DNA base is like a letter of the alphabet, and a sequence or chain of bases can be thought of as forming a certain message. This strand of letters, or message, is called a gene. The gene is the most basic unit of inheritance. Genes are coded to carry information that allows an organism to make the protein it requires. These proteins give the organism its character traits: how it looks, what it does, and how it behaves. Genes are strung together and tightly packed into coiled structures in the nucleus of each cell, called chromosomes. Every human cell has forty-six chromosomes, or two pairs of twenty-three chromosomes. One set comes from a person's mother, the other from the person's father. These chromosomes determine sex, physical traits, and other inherited characteristics of the individual.

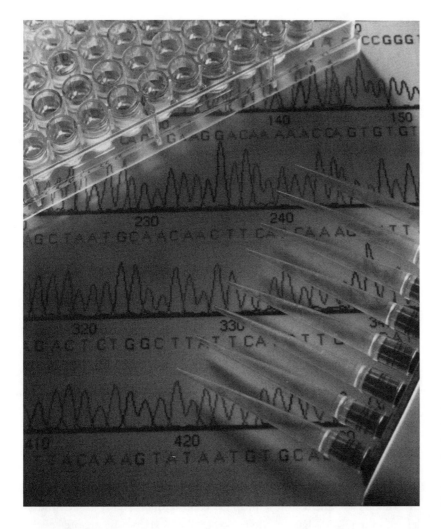

A printout of the basic sequence of DNA, which consists of four different types of nucleotides: adenin (A), thymine (T), guanine (G), and cytosine (C). PHOTO RESEARCHERS, INC.

Project goals

The Human Genome Project outlined several goals at the outset. One was to identify and sequence (find the precise order of the nucleotides) the genes. Because it is estimated that there are roughly 3.9 billion nucleotide bases that make up the human genome, identifying ways to store this information on publicly accessible databases was an important challenge. Another goal was to improve analytical tools so that sequences of the human genome could be compared to sequences from other organisms on special databases. Another important objective was to address the inevitable ethical, legal, and social implications (called ELSI in the project) of being able to map out an individual's genetic information.

The size of the human genome

To get some idea about how much information is packed into a tiny human genome, a single large gene may consist of tens of thousands of nucleotides or bases, and a single chromosome may contain as many as one million nucleotide base pairs and four thousand genes. The Human Genome Project Information Web site (http://www.ornl.gov/sci/techre-sources/Human_Genome/home.shtml) provides another way of looking at the size of the human genome present in each of a human's cells: "If the DNA sequence of the human genome was compiled in books, 200 volumes the size of the Manhattan telephone book (which is 1,000 pages) would be needed to hold it all. It would take 9.5 years to read it aloud without stopping." Even simply storing this information on a computer presented a huge challenge. In 1998, a private company, Celera Genomics, announced plans to sequence the human genome on its own, using the largest civilian supercomputer ever made to produce the needed sequences. The company agreed to cooperate with the governmental project.

Early success

The Human Genome Project made unexpected progress in its early years. In December 1999, an international team announced that it had achieved a scientific milestone by compiling the entire code of a complete human chromosome for the first time. Researchers chose chromosome 22 (one of the twenty-three pairs of chromosomes found in humans) because of its relatively small size and its link to many major diseases. The sequence they compiled is more than twenty-three million letters in length. What was described as the "text" of one chapter of the twenty-three-volume human genetic instruction book was therefore completed.

In 2000, the Human Genome Project gave the public its first news of the completion of the "draft sequence"—a rough draft of the human genome, with about 90 percent of the sequence. In February 2001, scientists working on the project published the first interpretations of the human genome sequence. Previously, many in the scientific community had believed that the number of human genes totaled about 100,000. But the new findings surprised everyone: Both research groups said they could find only about 30,000 human genes. This meant that humans have remarkably few genes—a little more than twice as many as a fruit fly, which has 13,601. This discovery led scientists to conclude that human complexity does not come from a sheer quantity of genes but from their structure and the way they connect.

By its own definition, the Human Genome Project was almost complete in April 2003, and the sequence of the last chromosome was published in May 2006. Some highly repetitive DNA sequences had not been sequenced, and knowledge about the functions and regulation of genes remained incomplete, but the genome sequence was, for all intents and purposes, complete.

Purposes of the project

With the genome mapped and fully sequenced, biologists were able for the first time to stand back and look at each chromosome as well as the overall human blueprint. They could begin to understand how a chromosome is organized, where the genes are located, how they express themselves, how they are duplicated and inherited, and how disease-causing mutations occur.

The genetic mapping led to the development of new therapies for diseases thought to be incurable. Detailed genome maps allow researchers to seek and find the genes that are associated with diseases such as inherited colon and breast cancer and Alzheimer's disease. Not only will doctors be able to diagnose these conditions at a much earlier point, but they also will have new types of drugs as well as new techniques and therapies that allow them to cure or even prevent a disease.

There are other uses for genome maps. In forensic science (the use of scientific methods to investigate a crime and to prepare evidence), for example, genome mapping makes it possible to create a DNA profile of a person with the assurance that there is an extremely small chance that another individual has the exact same "DNA fingerprint." This allows police to identify suspects whose DNA may match evidence left at a crime scene, and it can prove innocent those who have been wrongly accused or convicted. DNA fingerprinting can also determine whether a man is the father of a child and better match organ donors with recipients.

A deeper genetic understanding of plants and animals, as well as humans, allows farmers to develop crops that can better resist disease, insects, and drought. "Bioengineered" food is controversial because it adds human engineered genes into the environment with unknown results.

But it also enables farmers to use little or no pesticides on fruit and vegetable crops and reduces waste.

Other questions about the appropriate uses of the genome await answers. For example, what if health-insurance companies could test potential customers for future genetic diseases? What if potential employers could? How would an individual be affected by knowing his or her genetic differences?

Once completed, the Human Genome Project began to have a major impact on the life sciences and the quality of human life and health almost immediately. A highly successful effort by any scientific standards, it marks only the beginning of a better understanding of the genetic secrets of life.

Anne Hutchinson

Anne Hutchinson was a member of the **Massachusetts Bay Colony** from 1634 to 1637. She was an active community leader whose religious views differed from those of the leaders of the colony. After two trials, she was banished, or forced to leave, from the settlement. She and some of her followers founded a colony in the present area of Portsmouth, **Rhode Island**, where they could have religious freedom.

Early life

Anne Marbury Hutchinson was born in Alford, Lincolnshire, England. The date of her birth remains unknown, but she was baptized on July 20, 1591. Her father, Francis Marbury (1556–c. 1610), was a clergyman who was influenced by Puritan ideas. **Puritans** believed that the Anglican Church, the official church of England, should be simplified and cleansed of unnecessary rituals. Marbury got into trouble with the Anglican Church more than once for his beliefs. Hutchinson's mother, Bridget Dryden (1570–1644), was Marbury's second wife. In 1605, the family moved to London.

Anne Hutchinson received a better education from her father than most girls of the time. She was especially well educated in the scriptures of the Bible. In 1612, she married William Hutchinson (1586–1642), the son of a successful merchant. They resided in Alford, and over the course of their marriage, they had more than a dozen children.

The Hutchinsons participated in the religious meetings of the Puritan movement in Alford. They followed the teachings of Reverend John Cotton (1585–1652), who was forced out of his ministry in 1633 for his Puritan beliefs. He therefore left England to accept a position with the Boston Church in the Massachusetts Bay Colony. Anne and William Hutchinson decided to follow him there with their family in 1634.

Leadership and dissent

Anne Hutchinson quickly became a well-respected member of the community established in New England. Her intellect and kindness were well noted. As a woman, however, her activities were limited. She began hosting a weekly meeting for women at her home. The previous Sunday's sermon would be discussed. Her audience grew, and men began to attend meetings as well.

Eventually, Hutchinson moved beyond scriptural discussions and included discussions of religious philosophy. She embraced a religious view that was different than that of the church leaders. The Puritans generally believed in a covenant of works, which meant that a person had to obey church and scriptural guidance to gain access to heaven. Anne Hutchinson instead taught a covenant of grace. She believed that God's grace and love were revealed through personal intuition to those predestined to heaven. Her beliefs challenged the role of ministers and the church. According to her critics, Hutchinson's philosophies meant that no one had to act morally, so they felt that her teachings threatened the purity of the colony.

At first, Hutchinson enjoyed a large and supportive following. When one of her greatest critics, John Winthrop (1588–1649), was elected governor in 1637, much of that support was lost. The General Court, or government of the colony, banished one of her supporting ministers and sought to bring Hutchinson to trial. The charge related to misleading ministers and their ministry.

Anne defended herself against her accusers with strong arguments. Her confession, however, that she received direct revelations from God for one of her statements was heretical (against accepted beliefs). Puritans believed that God only spoke to humans through the Bible, so Anne Hutchinson was banished from the community. Refusing to take back her statements, she was formally excommunicated, or dismissed, from the church.

Later years

After the trials in 1638, Anne Hutchinson moved with her family to a new settlement in Rhode Island. William Hutchinson died in 1642, and Anne moved again. This time she settled with some of her family in the area of Pelham Bay, **New York**. In the late summer of 1643, Indians attacked. Hutchinson and all of her household, except one child, were killed. Many of her critics viewed the incident as proof of God's judgment against her teachings.

I

Idaho

Idaho joined the Union as the forty-third state on July 3, 1890. Situated in the northwestern United States, Idaho is the smallest of the eight Rocky Mountain states and thirteenth in size among the fifty states. It is bordered by Canada, **Montana**, **Wyoming**, **Utah**, **Nevada**, **Oregon**, and **Washington**.

Several Native American tribes lived in the region of Idaho when fur trappers and missionaries arrived in the early 1800s. The **Oregon Trail** opened in 1842, and pioneers used it for twenty years to pass through Idaho on their way to other points west. In 1860, gold was discovered in northern Idaho, and a gold rush ensued, lasting several years. (See **California Gold Rush**.) This led directly to the organizing of the Idaho Territory on July 10, 1863.

Between 1870 and 1880, Idaho's population nearly doubled. This white settlement threatened the Native American way of life and set off a series of wars in the late 1870s. The Nez Perce War is the most famous of the battles.

Idaho enjoyed an economic boom beginning in 1906 due to the completion of the country's biggest sawmill in Potlatch. With construction of this sawmill came the birth of the modern timber industry. By **World War I** (1914–18), agriculture was the state's leading enterprise.

As the twenty-first century progressed, Idaho experienced population expansion and the push for economic development. Both factors were in direct conflict with a new interest in the environment, and Idaho's leaders found themselves at odds regarding land use, mineral development, and water supply.

In 2006. Idaho was home to nearly 1.5 million people, 91.8 percent of them white. Boise, the capital, was the most heavily populated by far. The Nez Perce live in the northern region of the state on reservation land. The primary religion of Idaho is Mormon, and the Mormon population is second only to that in Utah. (See **Church of Jesus Christ of Latter-day Saints**.)

Idaho is not a wealthy state. In 2004, the average personal income was just under $27,000, far below the national average of $33,050. Many of the state's workers are employed in agriculture. Idaho's most famous crop is the russet potato, but it also grows sugar beets, barley, and hops.

Illinois

Illinois, also known as the Land of Lincoln, was the twenty-first state to join the Union, when it was admitted on December 3, 1818. It lies in the eastern north-central United States and is surrounded by **Wisconsin**, **Iowa**, **Missouri**, **Kentucky**, **Indiana**, and Lake Michigan. Springfield is the state's capital, but Chicago is Illinois's most heavily populated city, with nearly three million residents.

European explorers arrived in Illinois in the 1600s and found a number of Native American tribes living there. Tribal populations were decimated by European-induced disease, alcohol, and warfare. After the Black Hawk War in 1832, all remaining tribal members were forced to leave Illinois and relocate across the Mississippi River.

Half of all men living in Illinois served in the American **Civil War** (1861–65). The state had a deep-seated loyalty to President **Abraham Lincoln** (1809–1865; served 1861–65), a longtime resident.

After the **Union** victory in the war, Illinois experienced economic and population growth. Chicago became the major city of the Midwest. The completion of the Transcontinental Railroad in 1869 presented business opportunities never before realized, and small towns and cities built banks, grain elevators, factories, and retail shops.

The second half of the nineteenth century was the setting for the **labor movement**, a time when workers formally organized into unions, such as the **Knights of Labor**, in order to advocate for better pay and working conditions. Illinois was the center of this activity because it was a highly industrialized state. The Haymarket Riot of 1886 and the violent **Pullman Strike** in 1894 left scores of people injured or dead. In 1871, the Great Chicago Fire destroyed the city's downtown area. Its wealthy citizens took it upon themselves to rebuild their city, and their visionary attitude made Chicago one of the greatest metropolitan areas of the world.

The majority of Illinois enjoyed thirty years of prosperity in the first half of the twentieth century. Hundreds of thousands of immigrants moved to Chicago, most of them without money or jobs, many unable to speak English. In the 1920s, the city earned a reputation for violence and corruption as **organized crime** took hold. The **Great Depression** (1929–41) hit agricultural areas first. Industries began closing their doors and did not fully recover until **World War II** (1939–45) was over.

Illinois was hit hard by a severe recession in the 1980s; industrial workers were laid off indefinitely, and many of the jobs were permanently lost to automation. In 1990, Illinois suffered an unemployment rate of 7.2 percent, a full two points higher than the national average of 5.2 percent.

In 2003, Illinois had a $5 billion budget deficit, the worst in twenty years. By 2006, the state was developing programs aimed at creating jobs, providing healthcare, and increasing education funding.

Illinois's population in 2006 was just under twelve million, making it the fifth-largest among the fifty states. Of these residents, 72.2 percent were white and 14.5 percent were of African American heritage. The state remained ethnically diverse and claimed the sixth-highest Asian population in the nation.

Illinois's economy depends heavily upon human services industries such as law, education, finance, government, and business. Prior to 1972, meat-packing was the state's most famous industry, but that changed after the closing of the Chicago stockyards. Manufacturing, though concentrated in Chicago, is prevalent throughout the state.

Illinois boasts one of the better-than-average literacy rates in the nation, and Chicago is one of the leading arts centers in the Midwest. The state's library system is unusually strong; at the end of fiscal year 2001, there were 629 public libraries. Illinois boasts 277 museums and historic sites, including the Museum of Science and Industry, which attracts two million visitors each year.

Immigration

Immigration, the leaving of one's homeland to build a life in another country, was not a new concept by the late 1800s. Foreigners had been leaving their homelands for the United States for decades before. Immigration historians generally divide immigration into three waves. The first wave crossed the Atlantic Ocean from 1815 to 1860; the second between 1860 and 1890. Immigrants of the first two waves were mostly British, Irish, German, Scandinavian, and Dutch. The third wave crossed between 1890 and 1914. Immigrants of the third wave came primarily from Greece, Turkey, Italy, Russia, Austria-Hungary, and Romania. (See also **Asian Immigration**; **French and Dutch Immigration**; **German Immigration**; **Irish Immigration**; **Italian and Greek Immigration**; **Mexican Immigration**; and **Scots and Scotch-Irish Immigration**.)

Immigration to the United States was a process, not an event. It did not have an actual "start" date, nor will it have an "end" date. Still, immigration reached its peak from 1900 to 1915 when nearly fifteen million people entered the United States. That is as many as in the previous forty years combined. This influx (flowing in) of foreigners to the shores of the United States changed the nation's face forever.

Immigration records

Although immigration records dating back to the nineteenth century do exist, the numbers are not accurate either in terms of how many immigrants arrived in the United States or their ethnicity. This is so for a number of reasons.

Ellis Island in **New York** harbor was the major port (point of entry) for immigrants crossing the Atlantic Ocean to the United States. However, it was not the only port. Smaller ports dotted the shoreline, but those ports did not keep consistent or reliable records. The same can be said of overland immigrants from Canada and Mexico; some immigrants were counted, others were not. Chinese immigrants landed at a port called Angel Island in **California**.

Even after the immigration procedures were in place, immigrants were recorded according to their presumed nationality, not their ethnicity. This gives a distorted picture of who was coming to the United States. For example, sizable portions of the millions of people emigrating

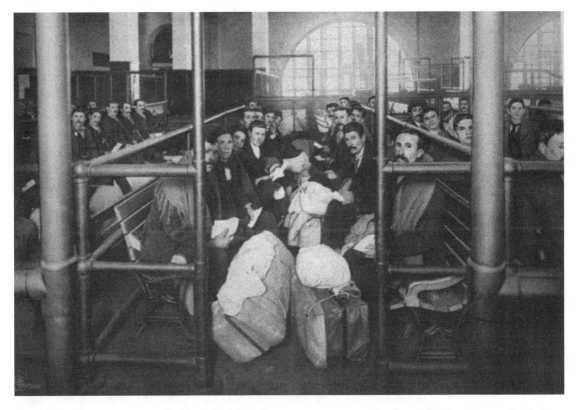

Hundreds of immigrants wait at Ellis Island through the long immigration process. People were forced to give every detail of their lives and pass a rigorous health inspection. THE LIBRARY OF CONGRESS

from Britain were Irish. But because they came from Britain, they were recorded as British, not Irish. The only Irish in the records were those from Ireland. Likewise, "Jewish" was not a recognized ethnicity until after 1948. (See **Jewish Immigration**.) Before that, the word referred only to a person's religious belief. So the number of Jewish immigrants was highly underreported.

The immigration process

First- and second-class immigrants—those who paid more for their tickets and so had access to better accommodations—passed through Ellis Island easily. Only the lowest classes (working class and most immigrants) were forced to endure a rigorous inspection. Even if these foreigners had nothing to hide, the process was stressful.

Immigrants were asked to give their names, ages, country of origin, and legal status in that country. Because many immigrants had last names that were difficult for inspectors to pronounce and spell, a great number of them were given new, more Americanized, names for their new lives. For people to whom family tradition held great value, this enforced name change was devastating.

After giving their occupation and work history, immigrants were asked questions about their religious and political beliefs. A health inspection followed this inquiry, and this was probably the most worrisome aspect of the process because immigrants had just spent months on board ships full of filth and disease. Many of the passengers left the ships ill. Immigrants were marked according to their condition: "P" indicated a pregnant woman; "X" was given to the mentally disabled. Anyone incurably ill was deported (sent home) immediately.

Immigrants who successfully cleared the inspection process then took an oath of loyalty to the United States and were allowed to enter. Where they went from Ellis Island depended on the plans they had made before the trip. A great many of them simply stayed in New York, at least temporarily, until they found work and saved money to move on.

At the peak of immigration in the early years of the twentieth century, immigrants accounted for almost one-third of the United States's population growth.

Coming to America

Contrary to popular myth, most immigrants of this era were not the poorest people in their society. They paid their own way or had their journey funded by a relative, a friend, or even a prospective employer. Most of these immigrants were young adult males, single or married with wives back home, who planned to work in the United States for a few years, save money, and return home. Immigrants who did not plan to stay in the United States permanently were called sojourners. Other immigrants, usually single women or men with families in the United States, stayed permanently. Plans often depended on the immigrant's experience in the United States.

Again, recordkeeping was not consistent, and statistics of those who returned to their country of origin were not kept until 1909. It is impossible to know, therefore, how many immigrants were sojourners who returned to the United States time and again.

Although each immigrant had his or her own individual reasons for emigrating, the primary reasons for leaving home, regardless of region, were economic, political, or religious.

The long voyage

European immigrants had to cross the Atlantic Ocean to reach the United States. Prior to the mid-1850s, the only method of transportation was a sailing ship. The trip took anywhere from one to three months, and it was a voyage of great discomfort.

Sailing ships were designed to carry cargo, not passengers. Captains, intent on making a profit by crowding as many passengers on board as possible, did little to adapt their ships. Flour, potatoes, tea, oatmeal, and maybe fish were provided. Water was provided too, but often it was stored in containers previously used to store oil and other liquids not intended for human consumption. Drinking that water put one's health at great risk.

Passengers often had only a few square feet of space per person. Narrow beds similar to bunk beds were poorly constructed, with a focus on quick dismantling rather than on comfort. There were no toilets or windows, which made sanitation a major problem. Passengers relieved themselves on deck, a habit that made conditions even worse. When a storm would hit, the ship would violently pitch, tossing around food, passengers, human waste, and anything else that was not secured to the deck.

Epidemics (widespread outbreaks of disease) were common and were the primary cause of death on immigrant ships. Typhus, a disease spread by head lice, was fatal if left untreated. Cholera was another deadly disease. Caused by infected drinking water, cholera victims became dehydrated to the point of death. Bodies were either thrown overboard or left on deck until the ship reached shore.

With the invention of the steamship came a shorter, more comfortable trip for immigrants. By 1867, the journey took just fourteen days; within forty years, that time was shortened to five-and-one-half days. The new ships were built specifically to carry passengers. Permanent beds were provided, and improved boilers allowed for reliable heating during the colder months. Health risks were greatly reduced as well, and by the early twentieth century the average number of deaths at sea was less than

1 percent of all immigrants. Ships could hold around three hundred passengers in first class and another thousand in steerage (the bottom level of the ship, always the least expensive fare).

During the 1880s, the immigrant trade became fiercely competitive. By 1882, there were forty-eight steamship companies fighting each other for business. All these companies were German- or British-owned; the United States never managed to break into this particular industry. The competition, however, worked in the favor of the immigrants for a short time. In 1875, rates on one of the most popular steamship lines were as low as $20 (steerage) and as high as $300 (first class). By the early 1880s, fares were reduced in order to attract passengers and could be bought for $10 to $20. This is the equivalent of about $200 to $400 in modern currency. Company owners soon conducted business the same way the railroads did, by forming "pools" and fixing prices so that no one company could undersell another.

Steamship companies brought immigrants to the United States, but the railroads were responsible for providing the motivation to make the journey. They owned thousands of acres of land—in northwestern states and territories in particular—they no longer wanted and could provide immigrants something other promotional agencies could not: transportation to get to the land, and the opportunity to buy the land once they arrived. The railroads published booklets advertising the United States and making offers too good to be true. They tempted immigrants with reduced transportation fees by land and sea, low-interest loans, classes in farming, and even the promise to build churches and schools. Some railroad lines assured immigrants that they would be hired for railroad construction at $30 a month plus board.

The South was interested in cheap labor to replace the slaves it had recently lost following the North's victory in the American **Civil War** (1861–65). (**Slavery** had been outlawed.) Immigrants, however, were not attracted to the southern United States because it had virtually no unsold land and very little large-scale industry. Without these attractions, immigrants would have difficulty finding shelter as well as work.

By the end of the nineteenth century, the railroads ended their recruitment campaigns. They had run out of land to sell at prices immigrants could afford.

New York City became an especially booming immigrant area, with little shops and food stands. AP IMAGES

What impact did they have?

Immigration was difficult for American and foreign workers alike. With millions of more people available, industries and businesses could hire employees to work for less money. Owners and managers knew people were desperate for work, and they took advantage of that fact by paying them low wages and forcing them to work in dirty, dangerous conditions.

But the greatest impact of immigration could be seen and felt in U.S. towns and cities. Rural America was disappearing as skyscrapers filled the horizon, and the **urbanization** of America was four times greater than the increase in the rural population in the late nineteenth century.

Cities could not be developed quick enough to keep up with the number of people who required housing. As a result, urban centers throughout the United States were overcrowded. This overcrowding led to unsafe living conditions and serious health issues. The immigrants fared the worst, as they poured into slums called **tenement housing**.

Immigration restrictions

Congress passed the first immigration restriction law in 1870. The Naturalization Act restricted citizenship to "white persons and persons of

African descent." Asian immigrants, then, were denied the right to become American citizens. The Chinese Exclusion Act was passed in 1882, further restricting Asian immigration. The Scott Act of 1888 forbid the return to the United States of any Chinese who had returned to their homeland when the Chinese Exclusion Act was enacted.

In 1891, a law was passed excluding convicts, the mentally retarded, the insane, the destitute (poorest of the poor), people with diseases, and polygamists (people with more than one spouse) from immigrating.

The Immigration Restriction League (IRL) formed in 1894 and encouraged Congress to pass a law requiring potential immigrants to take a reading and comprehension test. Although several presidents vetoed the bill, it finally passed in 1917. The law is still in effect in the twenty-first century.

Imperialism

Imperialism is the extension by a government of power or authority over areas outside the controlling nation. It results in the imposition of one nation's ways on another, creating an unequal relationship.

The imperialist extension of power is usually achieved through expansionism—acquiring or seizing territory. In the nineteenth century, the United States was intent on expanding its territory and economic influence. The doctrine of **Manifest Destiny** held that America was destined to expand from the Atlantic Ocean to the Pacific Ocean. The United States's expansionist goals were achieved through acquisitions such as the **Louisiana Purchase** of 1803; the **Texas** annexation of 1845; the Mexican cession that resulted from the **Mexican-American War** (1846–48) and gave the United States **California**, **Nevada**, **Utah**, and parts of Texas, **Colorado**, **Arizona**, **New Mexico**, and **Wyoming**; and the annexation of **Hawaii** in 1898.

Throughout history, expansionist and imperialist aims have often overlapped. Both involve a sense of mission and national identity. A nation's confidence that it is superior to others can contribute to imperialist goals. For example, as white American settlers moved across the continent during the era of **westward expansion**, they believed they had the right to take land away from Native Americans and to force their ways on the native populations.

Imperialism differs from expansionism in that it denies the rights of citizenship to the people of the lands that have been imposed upon. In many instances, an imperialist country exploits native populations for cheap labor, thereby increasing its own wealth and power. A country trying to expand its land holdings is not necessarily interested in domination or exploitation.

Anti-imperialism

As America continued to expand in the belief that the greatness of a nation depended on its size and power, many Americans grew uncomfortable with the idea. They believed expansionism was too costly, and they objected to bringing nonwhite populations into the country. In 1899, a group of anti-imperialists formed the Anti-Imperialist League in direct response to the **Philippine-American War** (1899–1902), which occurred following the **Spanish-American War** (1898). As a result of that war, the United States had won control of the Philippine Islands, Puerto Rico, and Guam. Also known as the Philippine Insurrection, the conflict was one of the bloodiest wars of the era. Filipinos were not willing to accept the United States as their landlord or their boss, and anti-Imperialists agreed with them.

The league was established in Boston, **Massachusetts**, but it soon had a national membership of more than thirty thousand. Its members tended to hold liberal, progressive political views. Among them were writer **Samuel Clemens** (1835–1910), also known as Mark Twain, and millionaire industrialist **Andrew Carnegie** (1835–1919).

The U.S. government threatened to imprison antiwar activists, including league members, in 1900. By the time the insurrection ended in 1902, more than four thousand U.S. troops had lost their lives and more than two hundred thousand Filipino civilians (some historians estimate the figure as a half-million or more) had died as a result of violence or disease. The league was unsuccessful at preventing U.S. colonial rule over the Philippines, which continued for the next thirty years. The league disbanded in 1921, but the efforts of this early peace movement raised awareness of the uglier side of imperialism.

Caribbean and Latin America

After 1900, America turned its focus to the Caribbean and Central America. The **Panama Canal**, a manmade waterway designed as a passageway between the Atlantic and Pacific Oceans through Central America, opened for business on August 15, 1914. The United States had total control of the ten-mile waterway, which became a major military asset and helped America become the dominant power in Central America. By **World War I** (1914–18), Cuba, Panama, the Dominican Republic, Haiti, and Nicaragua were protectorates (nations in formal or informal agreement with the United States to accept military and political protection from them in exchange for specific obligations). Puerto Rico was a colony (a territory under immediate and total control of a more powerful nation).

The United States's participation in World War I led to a reluctance regarding overseas commitments. The U.S. government withdrew its troops from Caribbean and Central America nations, relaxing its control in the region. Yet in economic terms, the U.S. government continued to push American exports and foreign loans, which some historians labeled "open door imperialism."

World War II and the Cold War

The **Great Depression** (1929–41) refocused American attention on domestic concerns. Then, with the advent of **World War II** (1939–45), global matters again took center stage. The United States, together with its **allies**, Great Britain, France, the Soviet Union, China, and others, defeated Germany, Italy, and Japan. The cost was immense, and only the Soviet Union and the United States emerged with enhanced power.

These two superpowers entered into an era known as the **Cold War** (1945–91), during which they engaged in an intense political and economic rivalry. The United States began to wield its influence to a degree greater than ever before. It supported anticommunist regimes in Guatemala (1954) and Cuba (1961), and as a prevention tactic, intervened in the Dominican Republic in 1965. Throughout the **Vietnam War** (1954–75), which was an effort to prevent the Soviet Union from achieving communist control in the region, Southeast Asia relied heavily on the United States for military aid. The United States became involved in other initiatives in the Middle East and Africa. In politics and in the media, debates intensified as to whether the United States had become a global imperialist.

The global reach of the United States

In the second half of the twentieth century, the cultures of many nations around the world began to emulate American lifestyles, fashions, foods, and trends. American **movies** and television programs were enormously popular overseas, and foreign students flocked to American colleges and universities. By the twenty-first century, "Americanness" saturated the world. Some historians called this phenomenon cultural imperialism.

When the Soviet Union dissolved, bringing the Cold War to an end in 1991, America remained the lone superpower. In the late twentieth and early twenty-first centuries, the United States on several occasions deployed its forces overseas. It sent troops to Panama (1989) to protect the neutrality of the Panama Canal and depose the military leader, who had ties to drug trafficking. It sent troops to Somalia (1992), Haiti (1994), Bosnia (1995), and Kosovo (1999), primarily for humanitarian reasons. The Gulf War of 1991, following Iraqi leader Saddam Hussein's (1937–2006) invasion of Kuwait, involved sending more than five hundred thousand troops to Iraq in an effort to protect the world's oil supply. And in 2003, the United States led coalition forces into war in Iraq; the U.S. government's primary stated reasons for the **Iraq invasion** were to bring democracy to the ailing nation and to end the threat of **weapons of mass destruction** believed to have been developed and stored there, but which were not found. The war was a subject of intense political debate and controversy. For instance, a 2007 poll conducted in Iraq for several American and European media companies indicated that 50 percent of Iraqis felt things in their homeland before the U.S. invasion had been better, while 12 percent felt they had not changed. As of 2008, U.S. troops remain in Iraq.

Impressment

In the modern world, developed countries build militaries using voluntary recruiting practices or laws requiring service. Before the acceptance of such practices, many countries relied on the forced tactic of impressment. Through impressment, militaries forced people to serve for them.

Impressed men often came from prisons, taverns, and boardinghouses. Brutal discipline maintained their presence and services as needed.

In the early nineteenth century, impressment became a challenging diplomatic issue between the United States and Great Britain. The English believed that one could not change citizenship or allegiance to a country. This was contrary to the revolutionary American belief that an individual had a right to choose allegiance. As a result, British naval vessels began the practice of boarding American ships to impress sailors who they deemed to be British deserters.

The British rarely spent time checking whether the nationality of those impressed was in fact British. Nine times out of ten, the sailors taken were not British. It fell to the U.S. government, however, to prove each case individually. As many as ten thousand men were impressed by the British between 1787 and 1807.

The British practice of impressing American sailors soured relations between the two countries. Though the United States attempted several times to negotiate an agreement to end the practice, Great Britain refused to stop. Impressment was a leading issue that caused the **War of 1812** (1812–15) between the two countries. Both the War of 1812 and the need to acquire dependable service members led to the decline of impressment after 1815.

Indentured Servitude

Colonizing the New World required hard labor. Governments and investors who wanted to profit from the New World's resources needed people to build and run communities, farms, and trades. Indentured servitude, and then **slavery**, were the primary means of obtaining that labor.

In 1606, the Virginia Company first tried to attract settlers to the New World by offering company stock, or a share of the company's profits. The method failed when the company had no profits to share with the settlers after seven years.

In 1618, the Virginia Company tried attracting settlers using a new method called the headright system. For Englishmen who could pay for themselves and their families to travel to the New World, the company gave 50 acres (20 hectares) of land to the head of the family and additional land for every family member and servant he brought along. In exchange, the settler had to pay the company a share of profits he earned from the land. Headright systems were soon used by other companies throughout the New World, but it was difficult for the companies to collect all of their profits and difficult for the settlers to find enough labor to work the land.

Indentured servitude was a way to obtain labor for farming, production, and trade in the New World. Under the system, a landowner or producer paid to transport a person from Europe and to house, feed, and clothe him, usually for seven to fourteen years. In exchange, the person agreed to work for the landowner or producer for those years. At the end of the agreed on number of years, the person became a freeman and received from his former master a small amount of land, some money, tools of his trade, or just a set of clothes.

Many indentured servants could afford to travel to the New World but needed help establishing themselves once there. Most indentured servants came involuntarily as an alternative to punishment for crime or to escape debt or poverty. Many Germans came to the New World through a system called redemption. Under redemption, ship owners paid to transport German laborers to the New World and then sold them into servitude to redeem the cost of their passage.

The life of an indentured servant was hard. Servants had to do whatever work their masters required of them. Indentured servants, however, had more rights under the law than slaves. While some indentured servants had to extend their periods of service when they could not afford their freedom, others earned freedom after their period of service, an option unavailable to slaves who were held against their will for their entire lives.

Indentured servitude slowly came to an end in the nineteenth century. During the eighteenth century, slavery replaced servitude for operating plantations in the South, and during the nineteenth century, economies in the North, fueled by crafts, trades, and industry, attracted free labor from Europe as the cost of passage to the New World fell.

This Certificate of Indenture describes the conditions under which a former slave will be apprenticed to a farmer in 1794. Indentured servitude was a common way to obtain labor for farming, production, and trade in the New World. KEAN COLLECTION/HULTON ARCHIVE/GETTY IMAGES

Indian Affairs, Bureau of
See **Bureau of Indian Affairs**

Indian Appropriations Act

As people in the United States began migrating west in great numbers in the nineteenth century, the government found itself with a problem on its hands. In order to entice white citizens and immigrants to risk everything they owned to settle in the western territories, the government needed something to offer, so it offered land for a very low price, or completely free. But those lands were already occupied by Native Americans who had lived there for many generations.

Like other groups throughout history, Native Americans were viewed through prejudiced eyes. They were considered inferior to whites and were treated unfairly. The federal government saw them not only as individual people, but also as tribal nations. In general, the rights of Native Americans were determined by tribal membership rather than on an individual basis. Tribal membership was the cornerstone on which the Native American culture was built.

Although the government often dealt in treaties (formal agreements), it did not always abide by the treaty terms. By the second half of the nineteenth century, broken treaties had resulted in the capture of most Native American tribes. Their land was taken from them and they were forced to live on **Indian reservations**. The government continued to view them mostly as tribes rather than as individuals, although this position gave Native Americans partial control over laws that affected them.

The federal government realized that Native Americans drew strength from their tribal ties and memberships. On March 3, 1871, the Indian Appropriations Act was passed. This law ended treaty making between tribes and the federal government. Native Americans were stripped of their power and their strength because from that point on they were considered only as individuals. This increased the power and authority of the government and was one more step toward dismantling the tribal way of life for Native Americans.

Indian Reorganization Act

The Indian Reorganization Act was passed on June 18, 1934, as part of President **Franklin D. Roosevelt**'s (1882–1945; served 1933–45) **New Deal** legislation. It marked a great shift in federal policy toward American Indians. Previous legislation had worked to bring Indians into the mainstream culture and disempower tribal unity. The Indian Reorganization Act was the federal government's first attempt to preserve rather than destroy tribal cultures. It did so in part by restoring to the Indians some rights and lands the United States had taken.

In 1933, President Roosevelt appointed John Collier (1884–1968) commissioner of Indian Affairs. Under Collier's leadership, the **Bureau of Indian Affairs** reformed Indian policy. Native schools were improved, employment rose, and cultural identity was revived. The act further empowered tribes by increasing their powers of self-government. It stopped the process of allotting tribal lands to individuals and restored or replaced some Indian lands taken in the past. Tribal self-determination was encouraged through the opportunity to establish democratic local rule. Indians were encouraged to restore unique aspects of their spirituality, language, and culture.

Each federally recognized tribe was given the chance to accept or reject the provisions of the act. Over two-thirds of the tribes eventually accepted it. The full potential of the act, however, was never realized. A shortage of government funds during both the **Great Depression** (1929–41) and **World War II** (1939–45) hindered implementation of the act. At the end of the war, pressure to end services to American Indians prevented further government support. It was not until the late 1950s that the federal government again embraced the policies behind the Indian Reorganization Act.

Indian Reservations

Indian reservations are federally owned lands that have been protected in trusts for use by Native American tribes. Their roots go back to Puritan New England during the 1600s. Missionaries there created reservations to convert the Indians to Christianity and European lifestyles. Current reservations were created in the nineteenth century to force tribes to embrace American ways and to open the way for white expansion into the

West. Resisting extinction, tribes have used reservations as places for preserving their unique cultures and traditions.

Establishing the reservation system

With the **Louisiana Purchase** in 1803, the U.S. government started to create reservations in the West. The government hoped reservations would reduce conflict with the Indians as American society expanded. These reservations had vague boundaries, where tribes were allowed to live until they wanted to integrate into mainstream American life.

Policies became stricter in the rush of **westward expansion** from the 1840s to the 1880s. The federal government created more definite reservations, and all tribes were forced to move onto them. Reservations were designed to serve two main policies. Forcing Indians to relocate allowed white Americans to expand into new territory without fear of conflict with the natives. Concentrating tribes on undesirable land forced some Indians to abandon their traditions and cultures by entering American society for jobs. To encourage this result, policymakers instructed Indians in farming and other aspects of Euro-American-Christian civilization.

The reservation system was not easy to establish. Corruption within the federal Office of Indian Affairs (later renamed the **Bureau of Indian Affairs**) was a problem. Some tribes could not live successfully on the poor lands allotted to them and had to be relocated again. Native American tribes sometimes resisted relocation orders, so the government increasingly resorted to military action to establish reservations throughout the 1860s. By 1877, nearly every tribe lived in confinement on a reservation, but conflicts continued into the 1880s.

Assimilation (conformity) programs continued through the early decades of the 1900s. The **Dawes Severalty Act** of 1887 allowed reservation lands to be sold in individual plots to non-Indians. Native American languages, religious practices, ceremonies, arts and crafts, and governments dwindled. Few reservations were self-sufficient, and poverty reigned. Refusing to assimilate, some tribes struggled to maintain their way of life despite the challenges.

The new reservations

In 1933, John Collier (1884–1968) became the commissioner of the Office of Indian Affairs. Collier supported a reform movement to preserve traditional Indian culture and society. Reform included passage of the **Indian Reorganization Act** of 1934. The act changed government policy concerning reservations, giving tribes new authority to govern themselves. The power of self-government allowed tribes to take steps to preserve their cultures and traditions.

Today, reservations continue to remain under federal control, but most have their own democratic governments. Tribal governments provide health, educational, and social services, just as state and municipal governments do. Many Native Americans make a living from the natural resources of their lands and from tourism that spotlights their unique cultures. Most Native Americans, however, make a living at regular jobs the same way non–Native Americans do.

Problems, however, persist on Indian reservations. Unemployment rates are high, as are alcoholism and suicide rates. Native American health is often poor. These problems are the legacy of centuries of U.S. government policy toward American Indians. Although tribes struggle with these issues, many Indians take great pride in their heritage and are determined to revive and preserve their language, culture, and traditions on their reservation lands.

Indian Territory

The land that now forms most of the state of **Oklahoma** appears as "Indian Territory" on maps drawn in the 1800s. Created for resettlement of Indian (Native American) peoples removed from the East, Indian Territory eventually was home to members of tribes from across the nation. Indian Territory was dissolved with the creation of the present state of Oklahoma in 1907. Today, Oklahoma has the largest number of Native Americans and the greatest number of tribal nations of any state in the United States. More than sixty-seven nations exist in Oklahoma; twenty-nine of these are federally recognized Native American Nations.

The original idea

In 1825, Congress set aside for Indian use the country west of **Missouri** and **Arkansas** and east of Mexican territory. Closed to white settlement, it was first called Indian Country and then, by 1830, Indian Territory. Indian Territory arose from the tensions created by the **westward expansion** of white settlers into Native American lands. The federal government wished to remove Native Americans from their eastern homelands, opening those lands to white settlement and it also wanted to protect the relocated Indians from land-hungry whites. In giving Native Americans Indian Territory, the government assumed that Indian Territory would remain the far western edge of the United States.

Relocation begins

Some Native American peoples voluntarily moved to Indian Territory from the east. Cherokees known as the Old Settlers moved there in 1828. Then, in 1830 Congress passed the Indian Removal Act, which authorized negotiations and funds for the relocation of all southeastern tribes to Indian Territory, whether they were willing to go or not.

During the 1830s, tens of thousands of Choctaws, Chickasaws, Cherokees, Creeks, and Seminoles were removed from their homelands in **Mississippi**, **Alabama**, **Tennessee**, and **Georgia**. These groups, often called the Five Civilized Tribes, were marched forcibly from their homes. Thousands died in the harsh removal. The Choctaw and Chicasaw moved first. A large group of Cherokees, led by principal chief John Ross (1790–1866) resisted the removal. After trying to stop the forced relocation in the courts and failing, all but a small portion were rounded up by federal troops in 1838 and confined to holding camps. Ross then agreed to oversee the journey of his followers to join those already settled in the northeastern part of Indian Territory. Fiercest resistance came from the Seminoles (see **Seminole Wars**). After a protracted war in the swamps of **Florida**, all but a few had been forced westward by 1842.

Life in Indian Territory

In Indian Territory, the southeastern Native Americans established tribal governments, planted crops, and founded new schools. Customs of daily life, religions, and cultural traditions were transplanted from the eastern homes and adapted to the new setting.

Meanwhile, other eastern tribes were being pressed to move into Indian Territory. From New York came Senecas and others from the Iroquois Confederation. Out of the Great Lakes region and Ohio valley came Potawatomis, Shawnees, Delawares, Wyandots, Kickapoos, Miamis, and others. Quapaws were displaced from Arkansas. These groups were assigned lands immediately west of the Missouri border.

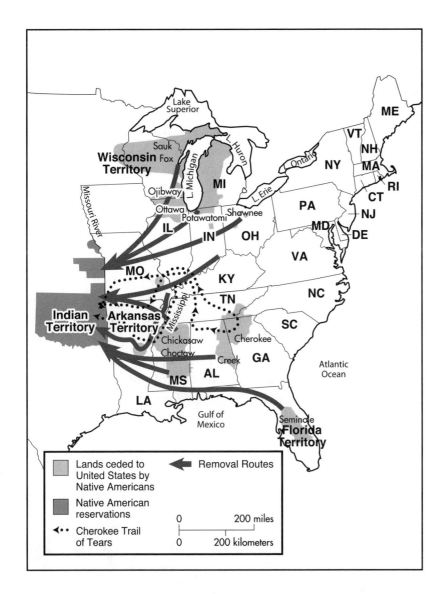

A map showing the lands given up by the Indians as well as their removal routes on their way to the new Indian Territory, which eventually became home to tribes across the nation. THE GALE GROUP

These relocations were mostly peaceful, except for a group of Sac and Fox people. Led by leader Black Hawk (1767–1838), this group resisted removal from Illinois, but after several bloody encounters with state militiamen, they were forced to resettle in **Iowa**, then part of Indian Territory.

In the 1840s, the U.S. government settled the tribes within the hunting areas of other tribes, often placing them near their traditional enemies without regard to the conflicts that would arise. The war-like

Osages, Kiowas, and Comanches, for example, were especially vigorous in attacking the newcomers from the east. Creeks and Seminoles disagreed on treatment of African American slaves brought with them, and old hostilities were rekindled between Choctaws and Chickasaws. Boundary disputes arose between the Creek and Cherokees. Divisions among the Cherokees were especially bitter. Relations between the followers of John Ross, who had resisted being moved, and the minority Old Settlers, who had supported the removal treaty, erupted into violence.

A "permanent Indian frontier"

The government meanwhile established military posts throughout the territory to maintain peace among the tribes. They continued to promise that Indian Territory would be permanent keeping whites and Indians apart and allowing the native peoples to gradually learn the ways of the white culture.

Events of the mid-1840s changed the frontier idea. **Texas** was annexed in 1845; **Oregon** Territory was acquired from Great Britain in 1846; and Mexico ceded a vast area of the southwest to the United States in 1848. With the United States now stretching to the Pacific Ocean, Indian Territory suddenly was in the middle of the nation, not on its far edge. As white settlers pressed westward, around and through the territory, the tribes there soon faced a new set of demands.

Losing more land

During the 1850s, Indian holdings in the territory were reduced dramatically. The organization of the **Kansas** and **Nebraska** territories in 1854 lowered the Indian Territory's northern boundary, removing more than half of its former area. Tribes in Kansas and Nebraska were urged to surrender land to white settlers now swarming across the Missouri River. Within a year, nine tribes agreed to withdraw to a small portion of their holdings and to sell the rest.

After the American **Civil War** (1861–65), the federal government forced a new series of land cessions (surrenderings). In what has been called the "Second Trail of Tears," many smaller tribes were removed from what had been the territory's northern portion. The Osages, Kaws,

Poncas, Otoes, and Missouris were resettled on land surrendered by Cherokees. Iowas, Sac and Fox, Kickapoos, and Potawatomies were removed to land taken from Creeks and Seminoles.

Bleak years

As the **Native North Americans of the Great Plains** lost the Indian wars of the late 1860s, they were sent into the increasingly crowded Indian Territory—Cheyennes and Arapahoes in the west-central portion, and south of them the Comanches, Kiowas, and Eastern Apaches. These years were among the bleakest of Indian Territory's troubled history. Western tribes struggled with the hopeless demand that they take up farming on the semiarid high plains. Angry rivalries and bitter memories continued to foul relations among the Five Tribes. The eastern part of Indian Territory became a haven for outlaws.

Texas cattlemen began driving herds across Indian Territory to Kansas railheads, and by the 1870s ranchers were pasturing their animals on Indian lands. The Missouri, Kansas, and Texas Railroad was built southward across the territory by 1872, followed by the Atlantic and Pacific and a branch of the Atchison, Topeka, and Santa Fe. As these developments introduced thousands of whites to the area, pressure grew to open Indian lands to outside settlement. By 1894, an estimated 250,000 whites lived in the Indian Territory.

The **Dawes Severalty Act** (also known as the General Allotment Act) of 1887 provided for breaking up land collectively held by Indian tribes into individual holdings, or allotments, with the remainder opened to white settlement. When special commissioners tried to set this process in motion in Indian Territory, they were vigorously opposed by native leaders. Congress finally compelled the Five Tribes to comply, and their lands were distributed among those on the tribal rolls or set aside for town sites and schools. Meanwhile, federal courts had taken full jurisdiction in the territory, effectively ending tribal governments.

The land runs

In 1889, much of the land of the western portion of Indian Territory was distributed to non-Indians through a series of dramatic "land rushes" or "runs." In one run that year, at least fifty thousand persons—known as boomers—arrived at the scheduled land rush. When the cannon boomed, they dashed onto the lands designated as "unassigned" to take up claims. The largest of these land runs was in 1893, when a portion of former Cherokee land was overrun by more than one hundred thousand boomers.

The western half of the territory and a strip immediately north of the Texas panhandle were taken over by non-Indians and organized into Oklahoma Territory. The tribes in what remained of Indian Territory petitioned Congress to allow them to form the independent Indian state of Sequoyah. Congress refused. In 1907, with all tribal lands distributed, Indian Territory formally disappeared when Congress merged it with Oklahoma Territory to create the state of Oklahoma.

Indiana

Indiana, also known as the Hoosier State, was admitted into the Union on December 11, 1816, the nineteenth state to join. A small state, it ranks thirty-eighth in size among the fifty states and measures 36,185 square miles (93,719 square kilometers). Indiana is in the eastern north-central region of the United States and is bordered by **Ohio**, **Kentucky**, **Illinois**, **Michigan**, and Lake Michigan.

French explorers first visited Indiana in the 1670s. There they found Native Americans, probably the Miami and Potawatomi tribes. By 1765, Indiana was controlled by the English. The first town plotted was Clarksville, in 1784.

In 1816, Thomas Lincoln moved from Kentucky to Indiana, and his son, future U.S. president **Abraham Lincoln** (1809–1965; served 1861–65), spent his life there from the age of seven until he was twenty-one. Although Indiana was not the site of any battles during the American **Civil War** (1861–65), it did send some two hundred thousand soldiers off to fight. After the war, industry exploded in Indiana with the discovery of natural gas in 1886.

As America became enamored of the automobile, a racetrack for testing cars was built outside Indianapolis in 1908, and the now-famous 500-mile (805-kilometer) race on Memorial Day weekend, the Indianapolis 500, began three years later. U.S. Steel built a plant and a city to house its workers. This city is called Gary, and it grew rapidly with the onset of **World War I** (1914–18).

Indiana's population is primarily white (86.1 percent), with another 8.6 percent African American and 1.2 percent Asian. The capital city of Indianapolis is the largest, with a population of nearly eight hundred thousand.

The state's economy is divided between industry and agriculture, and it is a leader in both. In addition to providing natural resources such as coal, gas, and stone, Indiana is the site of heavy industrialization, especially steel. Eighty percent of the state's farmers live on their farms, while more than 55 percent have another occupation outside of farming.

The Indianapolis 500 is the state's biggest yearly sporting event, and it attracts crowds of over three hundred thousand spectators. No other sporting event in the world is attended by as many people. Other than auto racing, Indiana is known for its amateur basketball—both high school and college. The Fighting Irish football team from the University of Notre Dame competes as an independent team and has won twelve bowl games.

Industrial Revolution

The Industrial Revolution began in England in the early eighteenth century, and developed later in the United States, around the time of the **American Revolution** (1775–83). Over a period of about one hundred years, machines in the United States gradually replaced unaided human hands in accomplishing the nation's work. With the use of labor-saving machines, the nation was able to produce goods on a large scale, build factories and plants, transport large quantities of raw and manufactured goods, farm on a much grander scale, and establish corporations and management systems to accommodate large-scale production. Industry transformed the United States from a rural farming society into the wealthiest and most powerful nation in the world.

Industrial Revolution in England

During the seventeenth century, England had a dramatic increase in population. Its farming economy could not support the large numbers of people, and the poor were forced to move to the cities to seek work. The cities desperately needed larger food supplies to feed their growing

A map of the Northwest Territory, composed of the modern-day states of Michigan, Ohio, Indiana, Illinois, and Wisconsin, produced a large portion of the nation's crops. During the Industrial Revolution, new ways to transport these goods were developed and became vital to the industry. THE GRANGER COLLECTION, LTD.

populations. The answer to the problem appeared in the form of new designs for farm machinery that could do large amounts of work with fewer laborers.

Machinery was also providing jobs in the cities and towns of England, where many former farm laborers found work in the textile (cloth-making) industry. In earlier times, cloth had been spun and woven in people's homes, but in 1730 new machines were invented that sped up the pace of spinning thread and weaving material. Around 1771, English inventor Richard Arkwright (1732–1792) built a waterwheel-operated mill to power his spinning frame, and this was considered the world's first factory. (A factory is a building or group of buildings in which many people work to manufacture goods, generally with labor-saving machines powered by a central source.)

The steam engine was the vital new power source of the Industrial Revolution. A steam engine burns wood or other fuel to heat water into steam, which in turn becomes the power that turns the parts of the engine. Early steam engines were designed to pump water from the English mines in the seventeenth century. In 1765, Scottish engineer James Watt (1736–1819) improved the designs. Watt's new steam engine could be used to power mills, so factories no longer needed to be near a source of moving water to power a waterwheel. By the last decade of the eighteenth century, steam engine–powered factories were being built throughout England. Using steam engines, iron and steel production became a thriving new industry.

Early U.S. textile industry

In 1789, British textile mill supervisor Samuel Slater (1768–1835) secretly memorized the details of the Arkwright spinning factory and emigrated to the United States. Once there, he designed and built the machinery for a cotton mill in **Rhode Island**. The mill went into operation in 1793. By 1828, Slater owned three factory compounds in **Massachusetts**.

In 1810, Boston businessman Francis Cabot Lowell (1775–1817) visited England's textile mills. After returning home, he enlisted the aid of a skilled mechanic and created a water-powered textile mill. At **Lowell Mills**, for the first time in the United States, raw bales of **cotton** could be turned into bolts of cloth under one roof. Lowell's company went on to build a complete factory town in Lowell, Massachusetts. The new, mechanized textile industry prospered and grew, employing thousands of workers, mainly in the Northeast.

British textile worker Samuel Slater designed and built the machinery for a cotton mill in Rhode Island based on designs he saw in England. THE LIBRARY OF CONGRESS

Transportation

In the first years of the new nation, the majority of Americans lived within one hundred miles of the East Coast, but as the nineteenth century began, people began to migrate west. Farmers in the West needed manufactured goods from the East, and easterners needed the crops from the West and South. There were few roads, and it was expensive and time-consuming to transport goods. Building transportation systems in such a huge territory was a daunting project, but over the next fifty years, roads, canals, steamboats, and railroads spread throughout the nation.

In 1817, Congress authorized the construction of the National Road, also called the Cumberland Road, from western **Maryland** to the Ohio River at Wheeling, **Virginia**. It was the first road to run across the Appalachian Mountains and into the territory known as the Old Northwest, which was composed of the modern-day states of **Ohio**, **Indiana**, **Illinois**, **Michigan**, and **Wisconsin**. The Old Northwest Territory produced a large portion of the country's crops. The National Road was the largest single road-building project to occur before the twentieth century.

Most of the country relied not on roads, but on the nation's rivers to transport goods. In the first half of the nineteenth century, most of the produce grown in the Old Northwest Territory was carried to market by man-powered boats on the Ohio and Mississippi Rivers. In the 1830s, steamboats (boats powered by steam engines) crowded the inland waterways of the United States. They expanded trade to towns and cities located along the major waterways. Steamboat construction became a thriving industry.

Still, many of the best farming districts in the Old Northwest had no river access. Canals, man-made waterways built for inland transportation, seemed to provide a solution. In 1817, the state of **New York** approved the funding of the **Erie Canal**, a 363-mile canal linking Albany on the Hudson River with Buffalo, New York, on Lake Erie. Upon its completion in 1825, the Erie Canal was already carrying monumental traffic. It proved an inexpensive route for shipping goods from the West, such as lumber and grain, to the New York ports, and for bringing manufactured goods from the Northeast to the West. New towns and industries were quickly established along the canal and on the Great Lakes. Many states rushed to build their own canals, but railroads soon emerged to compete in the long-distance transportation business.

Steam locomotives had already developed in England when a group of businessmen in Baltimore, Maryland, decided to launch the first U.S. railway, the Baltimore and Ohio (B & O) in 1826. By the early 1850s, several railroads had established lines that allowed them to transport freight between the Great Lakes region and the East Coast, and new railroad construction projects developed across the eastern United States. The explosive growth of the **railroad industry** in the eastern states, coupled with the potential wealth in the country's western territories, convinced growing numbers of people that a railroad stretching from coast to coast should be built. The effort was hampered by the American **Civil War** (1861–65), but on May 10, 1869, the rail lines of the Central Pacific and the Union Pacific were finally joined in **Utah**, completing the transcontinental railroad.

Farming

In the beginning of the nineteenth century, the vast majority of Americans were farmers. For the nation to become industrialized, it was essential that most farmers run commercial farms—farms that produced large crops to be sold—rather than subsistence farms, which provided food only for the use of the farmer and his family. The nation's crops, particularly wheat and **cotton**, were needed to feed the working people in the cities and to provide the factories with materials for manufactured goods. There was enough farmland to meet the demand for these crops in the United States, but there were not enough laborers until mechanized farming was introduced.

Eli Whitney (1765–1825) brought mechanized farming to the United States with his **cotton gin**. The simple machine cleaned cottonseeds from cotton fibers fifty times faster than a worker could do it by hand. Soon, southern plantations and farms were supplying huge amounts of cotton to the new textile mills in the Northeast and to Europe. Other mechanized farm tools followed, such as the McCormick reaper and the steel plow.

The efficient new tools actually damaged the financial situations of many farming families in the 1880s and 1890s. Record crop yields resulted in lower prices while production costs increased, a combination that threw many farmers into debt. Farmers' alliances arose, calling for reform.

Robber barons

The United States's tremendous industrial and financial growth in the last decades of the nineteenth century was due in large part to the entrepreneurial boldness and business instincts of a number of industrial and financial tycoons who came to be known as **robber barons**. **J. P. Morgan** (1837–1913), **John D. Rockefeller** (1839–1937), Cornelius Vanderbilt (1794–1877), **Andrew Carnegie** (1835–1919), James J. Hill

(1838–1916), **Jay Gould** (1836–1892), and others guided their business interests to levels of profitability that had never been seen before.

The **monopolies** (exclusive controls over the production of a particular good or service) of the robber barons enabled them to eliminate less powerful competitors, raise prices, and subsequently realize huge profits that were pumped back into their businesses. In 1890, the **Sherman Antitrust Act** was enacted in an effort to curb the power of the robber barons. But these men and their huge companies continued to dominate the U.S. economy.

Life in the city

The rural farm culture of the United States gave way to urban industrial culture as manufacturing plants multiplied and cities mushroomed in size. The nation's urban population rose 400 percent between 1870 and 1910, creating an **urbanization of America**. Large numbers of farmers moved to the city after the agricultural depression of the 1870s and 1880s. Joining them were an increasing number of immigrants from eastern and southern Europe. All were seeking work.

Cities of the late nineteenth century generally grew without planning. Living conditions were often deplorable, with thousands of families forced to reside in slums that were breeding grounds for infectious diseases. Crime was rampant: In 1881, the homicide rate in the United States was 25 per million; in 1898, the rate had risen to 107 per million. **Child labor** was common as well; in 1900, as many as three million U.S. children were forced to work full-time to help support their families. Poverty was hard to escape for urban laborers. Layoffs were common; as much as 30 percent of the urban work force was out of work for some period of each year.

By the 1880s and 1890s, the gulf between social classes had dramatically widened. In cities such as New York and Chicago, the fabulously wealthy built huge, elaborate mansions that overlooked desperately poor slums. The term "**Gilded Age**," coined by writer **Samuel Clemens** (1835–1910), came into common usage to describe the corruption and the false glitter of the era's wealthy. Reform efforts at the end of the century began a slow process to relieve the worst aspects of the division between the laboring classes and the social elite.

Internet Revolution

Between 1993 and 1995, the World Wide Web (www, or the Web), a user-friendly information-sharing network system, quietly came into being and began to spread. In its first fifteen years, the Web reshaped U.S. communications, businesses, and politics, fueled worldwide economic growth, and became a central feature in the daily lives of more than a billion people.

The Internet age began in the 1960s, when computer specialists in Europe began to exchange information from a main computer to a remote terminal by breaking down data into small packets of information that could be reassembled at the receiving end. The system was called packet-switching. In 1968, the U.S. Department of Defense engaged scientists to create a national communications system. Experimenting with packet-switching, the government scientists eventually linked several computers over telephone lines to operate as a single system. The system was called the Advanced Research Projects Agency Network (ARPANET).

By 1983, research scientists extended the use of ARPANET to form the early Internet, a large network connecting the internal systems of some universities and laboratories. Users were able to exchange electronic mail (now known as e-mail) and data, access computers at other locations, and communicate through newsgroups (one-topic discussion groups) and bulletin boards (message-posting sites). These exchanges demanded advanced computer skills, and the Internet remained a mystery to those without training.

Berners-Lee invents the Web

In 1989, English scientist Tim Berners-Lee (1955–) began work on a system he would eventually call the World Wide Web. His goal was to make the Internet accessible to everyone. Berners-Lee designed a standard set of protocols,

Cyber cafes are popular forums in which people socialize and have public Internet access. OLEG NIKISHIN/GETTY IMAGES

English scientist Tim Berners-Lee created the World Wide Web to make the Internet accessible to everyone. AP IMAGES

rules that create an exact format, or pattern of arrangement, for communication between systems. Hypertext Transfer Protocol (HTTP) became the standard communications language on the Web. (Hypertext is any text that can link to documents in other locations. Photos and other images, sounds, and video with links are called hypermedia.)

The next crucial step in the creation of the Web was to establish a server—the computer program that stores information and delivers it in the form of Web pages from one computer to another. The first Web server in the United States, developed at the Stanford Linear Accelerator Center in Palo Alto, **California**, went live at the end of 1991. Finally, to read the Web, users needed browser software, a program used to view and interact with various types of Internet resources. Berners-Lee developed a text-based Web browser in 1992. With the protocols, server, and Web browser in place, the World Wide Web was available to the public.

The Web improves and spreads

Improvements to the Web made it increasingly simple to use. In 1993, Mosaic, a browser that adapted the graphics, familiar icons (picture symbols), and point-and-click methods, became available. Mosaic caught on immediately—two million users downloaded it within a year. A year later, one of Mosaic's creators devised Netscape Navigator, a highly successful Web browser that gave users more comfortable Web access. In 1995, Microsoft entered the competition with its Internet Explorer.

Simplicity of use immediately brought users to the Web. Internet service providers such as CompuServe, America Online (AOL), Netcom, and Prodigy arose rapidly to meet the enormous demand for servers to link people to the Internet.

Most people working on **personal computers** (PCs) at home used dial-up connections, which were slow and tied up their phone lines. The first broadband options (meaning "broad bandwidth," a high-capacity, two-way link between an end user and access network suppliers that provided greater speed than telephone connections) appeared in 1997, but it was not until the early 2000s that millions of homes and offices connected through broadband to the Web on a twenty-four-hour-a-day basis.

The economic boom

During the late 1990s, the United States began to experience an economic boom (upswing) largely due to the success of Web-related companies, which came to be known as dot-coms. Because of the excitement of investors in the new industry, stock prices of the dot-coms soared. (Stock is the value of a company divided into individual shares. When a company goes public, the public can purchase shares.) This caused even more investors to jump in.

In 1995, Netscape offered its stock in a public stock offering. The stock price soared to fantastically high levels, making the company's young founders instant millionaires. Other Web-related industry stocks skyrocketed as well. AOL bought CompuServe in 1998 and Netscape the following year, generating tremendous proceeds each time. In 1997, Yahoo! Inc. was nothing more than a Web search index. By 1999, so many advertisers and investors had jumped on the Yahoo! bandwagon, it had become a major media company worth tens of billions of dollars. The stock of online auction house eBay, one of a growing number of e-commerce companies, increased 2,000 percent in value in less than a year when it went public in 1998. Amazon.com, a seller of books and other merchandise online, was valued in the multibillions long before it made its first annual profit in 2004.

The dot-com bubble bursts

Many dot-com companies were founded by young, innovative people who became suddenly rich when their companies' stock prices rose. Their employees were typically recent college graduates, lured by high salaries, fun work environments, and the promise of owning shares in ever-soaring company stocks. Dot-coms did not stick to traditional business practices. They frequently offered their services to potential customers for free, hoping to grab a corner of the future market. Profit was not a priority in the short term; in fact, many dot-coms never made a dime.

In 2000, the enthusiasm of investors decreased and dot-com stock prices stopped rising. Dot-coms started laying off their staffs; some merged with competitors. By mid-2001, many were out of business, their stocks worthless. The strongest companies reviewed their practices, cut their budgets, and prepared to compete in a new economy.

Web 2.0 and its social environments

After the dot-com bubble burst, a second wave of Web industries arose, which came to be known as Web 2.0. The leader among them was a successful search engine called Google. (Search engines are software programs that help users locate Web sites. They use programs, called "spiders" or "robots, " that go out and collect information, which is then stored and indexed in the search engine's Web site databases.) Developed by two graduate students in 1998, Google started on a shoestring. Its first offices were in a garage and it was financed by money borrowed from family and friends. The simplicity of this streamlined search engine made it an immediate success. Like most Web companies of the new century, Google added advertising to its pages in 2000, making it a highly profitable business. By 2004, it was handling the vast majority of Web searches and was valued in the billions of dollars. It became common for users to say they were "googling" something, rather than simply "searching for" something.

Many of the second-generation Web sites featured shared platforms called "communities." Within the community, members could publicly express themselves and participate in exchanges. For example, by the turn of the century, blogs had emerged. A blog (derived from "Web log") is an online commentary written by a nonprofessional writer in journal style that allows readers to respond. By 2006, there were an estimated sixty million blogs worldwide; by some calculations, a blog was being published every second. Among many other popular Web 2.0 environments are MySpace, a social networking Web site with an estimated 154 million members; and YouTube, a Web site on which users can display videos. Wikipedia, the free online encyclopedia written and edited by its readers, grew into a several-million-article project. These and many other Web communities are credited with changing the nature of popular culture in the United States by challenging the domain of the entertainment industry and professional journalists with the voices of ordinary people.

Web 2.0 companies generally do not follow standard business patterns. Most do not immediately make a profit. Commonly, after a new Web company emerges with something to offer, one of the larger Web companies buys it—sometimes for a lot of money. In 2005–2006, Google purchased YouTube for $1.65 billion; eBay bought Skype, which provides free phone calls via the Internet, for $2.6 billion; and News Corp. bought MySpace for $580 million. During that time period alone, the Web grew more than it had during the entire dot-com boom.

Fifteen-year view of the Web

The World Wide Web celebrated its fifteenth birthday in 2006. An estimated 210 million people in the United States and well over 1 billion people worldwide were regular surfers of the 92-million-site network, and these numbers grow daily. Most businesses conduct at least some part of their operations online. Most people use the Web for everyday aspects of life, such as checking bank balances, accessing work documents from home, donating to political campaigns or charities, and listening to music. The Web also has fueled growth in the global economy, creating new industries that profit by controlling and distributing information rather than manufacturing goods. Much like railroads and electricity in the late nineteenth century, the Web has created a new economic era.

Interstate Commerce Act

In the 1870s, businesses and especially farmers relied on the railroads to transport goods across the country. Railroad companies understood this economic dependence, and they exploited their customers by charging them unnecessarily high shipping rates. Everyone knew the railroads were guilty of unfair business practices, but the government was reluctant to get involved in economic matters. The United States operated at the time under a general belief that businesses needed to control themselves and each other.

As nationwide frustration over the situation grew, Congress decided the time had come to interfere in business since it was obvious it could not regulate itself. On February 4, 1887, the Interstate Commerce Act was passed, 50–20. As a direct result of the law, the Interstate Commerce Commission (ICC) was formed. The ICC was the first federal regulatory agency. Its purpose was to address the issue of corruption in the **railroad industry**.

The ICC demanded that railroad shipping rates be reasonable and just. Rates had to be published so that customers could know ahead of time what to expect. Rebates were outlawed. Rebates were refunds given to shippers who gave the railroads a lot of business. A railroad company would give a business a certain percentage refund on its total shipping charge if that business used only that railroad. This policy worked well for big businesses that did a lot of shipping. It put the smaller businesses at a disadvantage, however, simply because they did not do enough business to receive the rebate.

Finally, the ICC made the railroads lessen the price differences between long and short hauls. Previously, railroads charged more to go shorter distances, even though it did not cost them any more to make those runs.

Although the idea behind the Interstate Commerce Act and the ICC was commendable, the agency was virtually powerless to set rates or punish those companies that violated the law. When all aspects of the policy were in place, nobody was happy. The railroad companies believed the government was too involved in their business, and farmers felt it was not involved enough. So while the law existed on paper, it did little to improve the reality of doing business with the railroads.

Invisible Man

The novel *Invisible Man*, by Ralph Ellison (1914–1994), was published in 1952. It spent sixteen weeks on the best-seller list and was awarded the National Book Award in 1953. Some critics deemed the book the most important novel to be published after **World War II** (1939–45).

Plot

The novel is set in the late 1920s and early 1930s in the South. The narrator, who is African American, says other people refuse to see him, and so he has gone underground to write the story of his "invisible" life. In an echo of his invisibility, he remains nameless throughout the book. When he gives a speech to a group of prominent white men, he is rewarded with a scholarship to a reputable African American college. However, to get that scholarship, he is forced to fight, blindfolded, in a boxing match against other African American youths. They are then made to run over an electrified rug.

Three years later, the narrator, now a college student, is asked to drive a wealthy white trustee of the college around campus. The narrator takes him to a bar that serves only African American men. A fight breaks out among a group of mentally imbalanced war veterans at the bar, and the white man faints. He is taken care of by one of the veterans, who claims to be a doctor. The veteran accuses both the narrator and the trustee of ignorance regarding race relations.

Back at college, the founder hears of the narrator's misadventures and expels him from the school. He writes seven letters of recommendation and sends him to New York City to find a job. There, the narrator is repeatedly turned away until he reaches the office of Mr. Emerson, another college trustee. Emerson tells the narrator that he has been duped; the letters actually describe the expelled student as dishonorable and unreliable. Emerson helps the narrator get a low-paying job at a paint factory whose main product is the color "optic white." The narrator gets into a fight and wakes up in the paint factory's hospital.

The white doctors use this newly arrived African American patient to conduct electric shock experiments. When the narrator is discharged, he collapses on the street. A woman named Mary takes him into her Harlem home and helps him nurture his sense of black heritage.

The narrator eventually takes a job with the Brotherhood, a political organization that supposedly helps the socially oppressed. To take the job, he is forced to change his name, leave Mary, and make a complete break from his past. He complies.

He is successful at his job, but one day he receives an anonymous warning to remember his place as a lowly African American in the Brotherhood. Shortly after that, he is accused of trying to use the organization to advance his own desire for recognition. He is moved to another post but eventually returns to Harlem. There he realizes that many African American members have left the Brotherhood because the Harlem community feels the group has betrayed their interests. He finds one of the youth leaders on a street corner, selling dolls. But this man does not have a permit to sell, and he is shot dead in front of the narrator. After giving a speech in which he calls the slain leader a hero, the narrator is sent back to a white leader to learn the new strategies for outreach in Harlem.

The narrator learns that the Brotherhood is not what it appears. The group believes individuals are just tools to be used in meeting the goals of the Brotherhood. The narrator decides to leave the group, but he becomes involved in an act of arson. While running to escape capture, he falls into a manhole. He remains underground, and begins to understand that one must remain true to one's self and beliefs and yet find a way to be responsible to the community at large.

Themes

The novel's main theme is that racism prohibits people from forging individual identities. As an African American man living in a racist society, the narrator finds that each community (or community within a community) has different ideas as to how he should behave and think. These imposed ideas prevent him from discovering who he is, and allow others to see him as they want to see him. Without his realizing it, he comes to live within the limitations set by others, forged out of prejudice. After his time living underground, he comes to understand that he will be proud of his racial heritage and make important contributions to society, which will force others to acknowledge him for the man he truly is. At the end of the novel, he says, "And my problem was that I always tried to go in everyone's way but my own. I have also been called one thing and then another while no one really wished to hear what I called myself. So after years of trying to adopt the opinions of others I finally rebelled. I am an invisible man."

Another theme is the danger of using stereotypes to fight other stereotypes. All African Americans in the book feel the imposed limitations of racism. The narrator tries to escape these impositions as an individual, but he meets others who believe that all African Americans should fight prejudice in the same way. Disagreement with the majority is taken as a betrayal of the entire race.

This theme is illustrated in a passage in which the narrator finds a coin bank at Mary's home, just before he decides to join the Brotherhood. The bank is a symbol for the hurtful racial stereotypes the narrator has spent his life trying to escape. "The cast-iron figure of a very black, red-lipped and wide-mouthed Negro … stared up at me from the floor, his face an enormous grin, his single large black hand held palm up before his chest." The bank symbolizes the African American man as an object whose sole purpose is to entertain and amuse.

Ellison's novel addressed the social realities of racism but also exposed the way racism corrodes a person's sense of self and outlook on existence.

Iowa

The Hawkeye State joined the Union as the twenty-ninth state on December 28, 1846. It is located in the western northcentral region of the United States and is surrounded by **Minnesota, Wisconsin, Illinois, Missouri, Nebraska,** and **South Dakota**.

The Woodland Indians were the first permanent settlers of the land. White men did not show up until June 1673, when explorer Louis Jolliet (1645–1700) and priest Jacques Marquette (1637–1675) arrived. The French controlled the region until 1762, at which time Spain took over. French emperor Napoléon Bonaparte (1769–1821) reclaimed the area in 1800, then sold it to America in 1803. Iowa became an independent territory in 1838.

In the first decade of the twenty-first century, Iowa was home to just under three million people, 93.5 percent of them white. Another 2.2 percent was African American and 1.5 percent was Asian. The most popular church of Iowans is the Evangelical Free Church, followed closely by the United Methodist Church and the Lutheran Church-Missouri Synod.

Iowa's economy is based on agriculture, though it boasts a large farm-centered manufacturing industry as well. Iowa is known for its livestock and meat products. Corn is grown nearly everywhere throughout the state; nearly nine-tenths of Iowa's land is dedicated to farming. Despite the fact that it is an agricultural state, the **labor movement** has not been strong there. In 2005, just 11.4 percent of employed wage and salary workers were members of labor unions.

Iowa is one of the most important states in the political arena because it always holds the first presidential caucus (gathering of voters to select delegates to the state convention). The caucus is held in January of the election year, and because the media gives Iowa's voters such intense coverage and attention, those voters have a great deal of influence over the rest of the nation's voters.

After the end of the American **Civil War** (1861–65), Iowa voters supported Republicans over Democrats until the 1930s, when they supported **Franklin D. Roosevelt** (1882–1945; served 1933–45) in two presidential elections. The years 1940 through 1984 saw them voting Republican once again, but Democrats carried the state in 1988, 1992, 1996, and 2000. The year 2004 saw them vote Republican again.

Iran-Contra Scandal

The year 1986 marked the beginning of a six-year period of revelations, prosecutions, publicized hearings, and special investigations that became known as the Iran-Contra scandal. Involved in the scandal were officials from the administrations of both **Ronald Reagan** (1911–2004; served 1981–89) and **George H. W. Bush** (1924–; served 1989–93).

The events leading to the scandal were put in place on October 5, 1986, when **Central Intelligence Agency** (CIA) cargo specialist Eugene Hasenfus (1941–) was shot down over Nicaragua and captured by Nicaraguan government forces. His aircraft was full of weapons intended for Nicaraguan rebels, known as Contras. The Contras were in a rebellion against the Nicaraguan government. Congress had passed laws in 1982 and 1984 expressly forbidding U.S. attempts to aid or arm the Contras. Hasenfus's capture was evidence that the Reagan administration had broken those laws.

Reagan initially denied having any connection to Hasenfus's flight, but his claims were later proven false. Within five weeks, a Lebanese newspaper revealed that Robert McFarlane (1937–), Reagan's special assistant for national security, had engaged in secret arms-for-hostages deals with the Iranian government. These hostages had been captured by Iran in 1983, and the official U.S. policy was never to make trades with terrorist governments. It would be revealed during the scandal that such trades had actually been ongoing for years. It also came to light that money obtained in secret arms movements to Iran was directly supporting the Contras, another violation of the law.

Conflicting stories

Reagan denied the validity of the arms sales reports in November but one week later admitted he lied. He still contended that the sales were not in exchange for hostages. Within one more week, the president said those sales were legal. According to the National Security Act, the president has the right to override a law legally if he issues a finding in which national security issues are claimed. Reagan claimed to have such a finding, but it was proven that the finding was signed to override the Arms Export Control Act only after the fact. In addition, Reagan never informed Congress of the finding until after the scandal was publicized.

Lietenant Colonel Oliver North (1943–) was a key figure in the covert operations involving the Contras. As the scandal was revealed, Reagan fired North, who was then summoned to testify in July 1987. During his testimony, North admitted he altered official National Security Act papers to cover for the president. He also admitted to shredding thousands of documents that would have incriminated himself and many others, including President Reagan. North testified that he believed Reagan was aware of and approved his actions. North's supervisor, Admiral John Poindexter (1936–), denied this. Several other Reagan administration officials testified and denied having any knowledge of hostage deals or transfers of arms and cash.

Investigations

The scandal prompted a number of investigations. The first was the Tower Commission, named after its chair, former U.S. senator John Tower (1925–1991) of **Texas**. Reagan appointed the commission to perform a comprehensive review of the National Security Council's role in the affair. The commission's report in 1987 blamed the council's staff and concluded the scandal was a result of the president's poor management skills. The public did not accept this excuse and demanded further investigation. Each house of Congress established its own investigative committee and held televised hearings throughout the summer of 1987. Their final conclusion lay the blame at the president's feet, not at North's or Poindexter's. The committees chose not to investigate numerous areas of concern that emerged from testimony, including allegations that

North was directly involved in narcotics operations with connections in the Central American governments.

Special Prosecutor Lawrence E. Walsh (1912–) carried out his own investigation and found that the Iran-Contra policies that led to the illegal activity were developed at the highest levels of the Reagan administration with the knowledge of every senior cabinet member involved in foreign policy. Walsh concluded that these officials deliberately misled Congress and the public.

Fourteen individuals were tried for criminal violations. North and Poindexter were found guilty, but their testimony granted them immunity against criminal prosecution. McFarlane received a short sentence, and many others escaped prosecution because the evidence was found too late to legally prosecute under the statutory limitations. President George H. W. Bush pardoned (formally forgave) two others in 1992.

Impact

After six years of scrutiny and investigation, very little was done to hold accountable those responsible for the scandal. This, on top of the fact that taxpayers spent tens of millions of dollars on the scandal, left much of the American public cynical about the government and its officials. In an ironic twist, North, whose involvement in the Iran-Contra scandal was proven and admitted at least to a certain degree, became something of a hero among conservatives. He wrote several best-selling books and is largely considered by that population to be a scapegoat (someone who takes the blame for others' actions) for the Reagan administration. North was permanently banned from Costa Rica for his alleged participation in drug trafficking to help fund the Contras.

Iran Hostage Crisis

Beginning in 1953, when the United States helped to overthrow the popular Iranian prime minister Mohammad Mosaddeq (1882–1967), Iran condemned the United States as an oppressive power that interfered in foreign governments. The United States supported the new, unpopular government in Iran, which only worsened the country's feelings toward the superpower.

Relations between the two countries were particularly strained in 1977. The Iranian economy, which had boomed between 1973 and

Iran radicals move one of the hostages during the 444-day Iran hostage crisis. The standoff ended on January 20, 1981, the day of Ronald Reagan's inauguration. MPI/HULTON ARCHIVE/GETTY IMAGES

1975, began to deteriorate rapidly. There was a huge gap in the distribution of income between those who lived in the country, who were wretchedly poor, and those in the cities. A shortage of skilled labor brought in workers from Korea, the United States, and the Philippines.

The bazaar (open marketplace where goods are sold in booths or stands) was the heart of Iran's economy, but in 1977, government-controlled inspectors prowled the streets looking for price gougers who sold items at hugely inflated prices. Those found were arrested and exiled. The government's corrupt schemes and policies kept the poor desperate.

In that same year, Islam became a powerful political force, and Iranians embraced the religion as a means of dealing with the tyranny of the government.

Conditions worsen

U.S. president **Jimmy Carter** (1924–; served 1977–81) was dedicated to human rights, not only for citizens of his homeland but also for people everywhere. In order to continue receiving military and financial support from the United States, Iran's shah (head of government, like a king), Mohammad Reza Pahlavi (1919–1980), implemented a reform program focused on land reform and literacy. Most Iranians felt the shah's efforts improved conditions only minimally, and they feared things would regress once he had won Carter's approval.

The shah and his henchmen responded to his critics with arrests and torture. Protests and demonstrations became common occurrences as the Iranian people refused to be oppressed any longer. Between January 1978 and February 1979, an estimated ten to twelve thousand people were killed, and another fifty thousand were injured by the shah's forces.

Because the United States supported the shah's violent regime, the Iranian citizens' anti-American sentiment increased. Conditions reached the lowest point when the corrupt shah left Iran and was granted refuge (safety) in New York City in October 1979 to receive some medical treatment. He had lost his country to the Ayatollah Ruhollah Khomeini (c. 1900–1989).

Hostages are taken

On November 4, 1979, a group of almost five hundred radical Iranian students stormed the U.S. embassy in Teheran and took hostage about ninety people. Most of them worked in the embassy, and sixty-six of them were U.S. citizens. The students held fifty-two of them hostage for 444 days. The hostages were poorly fed, placed in small cells, and ordered not to communicate. Those who broke the rules were locked in solitary confinement for as long as three days. Near the end of their captivity, the hostages were forced to stand before mock firing squads.

Most nations joined the United States in condemning the Iranian revolutionaries' actions. Carter underestimated the power of the Islamic revival, and his inability to get the hostages freed caused irreparable harm to his presidency. He never wavered in his support of the exiled shah, and when an attempt to rescue the hostages had to be aborted in April 1980, the president's popularity was permanently damaged.

Historians generally agree that the Iran hostage crisis was one of the primary reasons why **Republican Party** candidate **Ronald Reagan** (1911–2004; served 1981–89) won the 1980 presidential election by a landslide. On January 20, 1981, the day of Reagan's inauguration, the hostages were freed.

Before the hostage crisis, Iran had been a country shrouded in mystery. The wide media coverage of the crisis forced the United States and other countries to try to understand Iran and its people. Unfortunately, the crisis left a legacy of misunderstanding that would cripple Iranian-American relations for years.

From the point of view of the Iran revolutionaries, the hostage crisis enabled them to prove what they had been claiming all along: Once the embassy was seized, the militants found evidence that the United States had joined forces with the Soviet Union to back the Iranian government and oppose the revolution. In taking the hostages, they won the support of the masses and effectively ended any attempt the United States might have made to reverse the revolution.

Iraq Disarmament Crisis (1991–2003)

At the end of the **Persian Gulf War** in 1991, the United Nations (UN) Security Council (the UN department in charge of maintaining peace among nations) determined that Iraq presented a threat to other nations and must be disarmed. Over the next twelve years, the UN and other national groups sponsored a series of sanctions (measures that punish a country for not complying with international laws or policies) and weapons inspections designed to disarm Iraq. Iraq president Saddam Hussein (1937–2006) was generally hostile to these efforts, and conflicts arose.

An uneasy peace

Hussein had remained in power after the Gulf War, but other nations were troubled by his rule. Many Iraqis faced persecution and even death under his regime. Hussein also had obvious ambitions to control the Arab world. Most troubling to the United States was that the Iraqi government had invested heavily in its defense industry, particularly in the development of missiles (rockets that can carry nuclear or nonnuclear

United Nations workers seal leaks in Iraqi rockets that were reportedly filled with chemical nerve agents. AP IMAGES

bombs) and chemical weapons (toxic substances, such as nerve gas or mustard gas, that are specifically designed to cause death or other harm and usually require only small amounts to kill large numbers of people).

Prior to the Gulf War, the United Nations had placed an economic embargo (prohibition of trade with a country) on Iraq involving almost all foreign trade with the country. These sanctions remained in effect after the Gulf War until the UN could be sure that Iraq was complying with its disarmament requirements, particularly that it was no longer building **weapons of mass destruction** (WMD). These massive weapons can kill or incapacitate large numbers of people. In April 1991, the UN created a special commission, the United Nations Special Commission (UNSCOM), and announced that it would begin immediately to inspect Iraq for weapons of mass destruction. Under the UN sanctions, Iraq was given fifteen days to provide information on the location of all its WMD facilities. UNSCOM would then have four months to devise a plan for making certain that Iraq was in compliance with the resolution.

The UNSCOM inspectors officially worked for the UN, but most of them came from the United States, Great Britain, and other advanced industrialized countries. The fact that the inspectors were from the

West—Iraq's former military foe—made reaching an agreement between the inspectors and Iraq difficult. The project dragged on. Time and again, the Iraqi government refused to turn over information or allow the UNSCOM inspectors into certain facilities.

Effects of the sanctions

The sanctions placed on Iraq in 1990 and 1991 took a severe toll on Iraqi civilians. Before the Gulf War, Iraq had one of the most advanced economies in the Middle East. It got the money it needed to import food and other consumer goods primarily by selling its oil. Sanctions all but completely cut off the oil trade. One estimate suggests that Iraq lost about $130 billion in oil revenues during the 1990s, bringing intense poverty to many Iraqi civilians. By some estimates, approximately five hundred thousand people died directly or indirectly as a result of the economic sanctions. Some estimates put the total deaths at a million people. The sanctions hit Iraq's health care system particularly hard. Water purification supplies were not readily available, increasing exposure to cholera and other diseases. A 1997 UN report found that more than 10 percent of Iraqi children were acutely malnourished (suffered ill health due to an inadequate diet). The death rates for infants and children under five were more than twice what they had been before the Gulf War.

At the end of the Persian Gulf War in 1991, the UN and other national groups sponsored a series of sanctions and weapons inspections designed to disarm Iraq. In 1998, UN secretary-general Kofi Annan tried to work with Iraq to make the disarmament process run smoothly. FABRICE COFFRINI/AFP/GETTY IMAGES

Tensions increase

A series of incidents convinced the United States that Hussein was not going to comply with the disarmament. In January 1993, the United States accused Hussein of moving missiles into southern Iraq. Allied planes and ships destroyed the missile sites, as well as a nuclear facility outside Baghdad, Iraq. In June 1993, the United States learned of a plot to assassinate former U.S. president **George H. W. Bush** (1924–; served 1989–93). In response, U.S. ships attacked Iraqi intelligence headquarters in Baghdad. In 1994, Hussein moved Iraqi troops to the Kuwaiti border. The United States responded by deploying a carrier group, warplanes, and some fifty-four thousand troops. Then, in August 1996, Hussein invaded the Kurdish territory, an area of northern Iraq that was home to the Kurds, a group Hussein had suppressed. U.S. ships and planes attacked military targets in Iraq.

Tensions between Iraq and the U.S.-led allies escalated considerably in October 1997, when Iraq accused U.S. members of UNSCOM of being spies and forced most of them to leave the country. In November, Iraq expelled the six remaining U.S. inspectors, and the UN removed its last inspectors in protest. As the United States and Britain began a military buildup in the Persian Gulf, Iraq readmitted the inspectors, but later in November Iraqi officials announced that they would not allow inspection of sites designated as "palaces and official residences." Not surprisingly, these happened to be areas long suspected by the UN as being possible storage sites for weapons of mass destruction.

In February 1998, UN secretary general Kofi Annan (1938–) forged an agreement with Iraq to resume weapons inspections in return for a UN promise to consider ending sanctions. Inspections went on relatively uneventfully until August, at which point the Iraqi government, complaining that it had seen no UN effort to end sanctions, refused to cooperate further with weapons inspectors. U.S. and British governments warned of possible military action to force Iraqi compliance, and the countries built up forces in the Persian Gulf. Just as allied bombers were preparing to strike Iraq, Hussein agreed to readmit UNSCOM weapons inspectors. Still, the UNSCOM chief inspector reported on December 8, 1998, that Iraq was not cooperating, and the UN again withdrew its team.

Operation Desert Fox

Due to opposition from France, Russia, and China, as well as several Arab countries, the UN was not prepared to take military action against Iraq. So the United States and Britain did, launching Operation Desert Fox on the night of December 16, 1998. Air raids against military targets in Iraq continued for the next three nights. On December 21, the U.S. Department of Defense reported that the bombing had severely damaged forty-three targets, moderately damaged thirty others, and lightly damaged twelve more, while missing thirteen targets. The Iraqi government claimed that the bombing had killed about one hundred soldiers and many more civilians.

Though Operation Desert Fox was militarily successful, the United States was not enthusiastic. On December 18, midway through the bombing campaign, the U.S. House of Representatives voted to impeach U.S. president **Bill Clinton** (1946–; served 1993–2001) for committing perjury before a grand jury. Critics said he bombed Iraq to take the attention off his own political problems. Other critics maintained that the bombing did little to stop Iraqi militarization, leaving the problem smoldering, quite possibly to flare up at some other time.

After the Desert Fox bombings, the Iraqi government refused to cooperate with weapons inspectors and it was a year before the UN could put together a new inspections team, the United Nations Monitoring, Verification, and Inspection Commission (UNMOVIC). Hussein did not cooperate with UNMOVIC for two more years. According to most reports today, by that time, Iraq did not have weapons of mass destruction and did not pose a real threat to other nations. Despite the difficulties, during its time in Iraq UNSCOM discovered most of Iraq's weapons of mass destruction and destroyed them. Hussein, however, was unwilling to fully cooperate with the inspections to prove this. In the spring of 2003, the United States invaded Iraq (see **Iraq Invasion (2003)**).

Iraq Invasion (2003)

On March 20, 2003, the United States launched an attack on the nation of Iraq. U.S. president **George W. Bush** (1946–; served 2001–) and members of his administration claimed that Iraqi president Saddam Hussein (1937–2006) had been stockpiling **weapons of mass destruction**—massive nuclear, biological, or chemical weapons that can kill or

After the fall of Saddam Hussein, it has been extremely difficult to put together an Iraq government that represents the Shi'a, the Sunnis, and the Kurds. MIRRORPIX/GETTY IMAGES

incapacitate large numbers of people—in violation of the terms of the international agreements formed after the **Persian Gulf War** of 1991. The administration also claimed a link between Iraq and **al-Qaeda,** the organization responsible for the **September 11, 2001, terrorist attacks**.

Shock and awe

The United States was unable to win approval for an invasion of Iraq from the United Nations. Nonetheless, the Bush administration claimed that an invasion was justified by United Nations Resolution 1441, adopted in 2002, which requires complete disclosure of a country's programs to develop weapons of mass destruction.

Without the support of the United Nations, the United States put together a coalition of forces dominated by U.S. and British troops, with limited support from Australia, Denmark, Poland, and other nations, and drew up plans to invade. Some of the United States's traditional allies, including Canada, France, and Germany, refused to participate, arguing that the United Nations had determined that there was no evidence that Iraq had weapons of mass destruction. Worldwide opposition to the invasion was demonstrated in many popular protests between January and April 2003, the largest of which took place on February 15, 2003, when protests in more than eight hundred cities around the world drew between six and ten million people. In spite of these demonstrations of disapproval, the U.S. military assembled 125,000 troops in Kuwait; Britain assembled another 45,000.

On March 17, 2003, the coalition gave Hussein and his sons Uday and Qusay forty-eight hours to leave Iraq. On March 20, 2003, coalition forces proceeded to attack, bombing hundreds of targets in Iraq's capital, Baghdad, in Mosul, the second-largest city, and in the southern city of Kirkuk. Their plan was for a "shock and awe" attack—an intense bombing raid accompanied by a ground invasion, intended to overwhelm the Iraqi resistance and bring about the collapse of Hussein's government with a minimum number of casualties. Within three weeks, Iraq's military had collapsed and Hussein and his Ba'ath Party leaders had fled, and U.S. troops took over Baghdad.

On March 20, 2003, coalition forces led an intense bombing raid and ground invasion targeting areas in Iraq's capital, Baghdad. AP IMAGES

Once ground troops entered Iraq, repeated efforts failed to uncover any signs of weapons of mass destruction. Intelligence reports demonstrated there was never a link between Saddam Hussein and al-Qaeda.

Occupation

After overthrowing Hussein, the U.S.-led coalition began an occupation of Iraq (control of the country by military forces) in an attempt to stabilize the country while it put together a democratic government. Two months after the invasion, President Bush gave a dramatic "mission accomplished" speech to cheering troops on an aircraft carrier that had just returned from duty in Iraq. The speech declared a U.S. victory in the war, but fighting in Iraq had escalated after the overthrow of Hussein, and there were not enough coalition troops in the nation to stop the violence.

Insurgency

Muslims in Iraq, as elsewhere in the Muslim world, are divided into two major branches, Sunnis and Shi'a, which differ in their beliefs about the legitimacy of particular religious leaders. Over the years, they also have developed some different religious practices; hostilities between the two branches have at times been intense. Only 10 to 15 percent of the Muslim world is Shi'a, but Iraq has a majority (60 percent) Shi'a population. Hussein and his Ba'ath Party officials were members of the Sunni minority, and they led a secular (nonreligious) government in which the Sunni minority ruled over the Shi'a majority.

When Hussein was overthrown, conflict between the Sunnis and Shi'a broke out, and some members of both groups wanted a religious government rather than the secular democracy the United States had envisioned for them. Iraq is further divided by a third group, the Kurds, an ethnic group with origins in Kurdistan, the mountainous area around the borders of Iraq, Turkey, Iran, and Syria. They inhabit a large territory in northern Iraq and make up about one-fifth of Iraq's population. Most Kurds are Sunni, but some are Shi'a, and there are also Christian and Jewish Kurds. Kurds in Iraq have remained isolated from other Iraqis and were brutally repressed by successive Iraqi governments; they hope to form their own independent nation.

Although there was little indication of an al-Qaeda presence in Iraq before the invasion, by 2004 terrorist groups from outside Iraq had moved into the country. A Sunni militant group led by Jordanian Abu Musa al-Zarqawi (1966–2006) pledged its allegiance to al-Qaeda in October 2004. This group, which came to be known as Al-Qaeda in Iraq, claimed responsibility for bombings, suicide attacks, kidnappings, and televised beheadings of Iraqis and foreigners. One of their missions was to encourage the fighting between the Sunnis and Shi'a. They believed the chaos resulting from the civil war would prevent the formation of a western-style secular democracy and allow Sunni Muslims to take power.

The Abu Ghraib Scandal

In April 2004, photographs depicting U.S. soldiers' humiliation and abuse of Iraqi prisoners at Baghdad's Abu Ghraib prison were published in the international media. Prisoners alleged that they had been tortured and assaulted by their guards and by members of the **Central Intelligence Agency** (CIA). In the scandal that followed, the U.S. commander of the prison was demoted, and seventeen soldiers were removed from duty; two of them were convicted and imprisoned for their roles in the assaults. Abu Ghraib prison was handed over to the Iraqi government in September 2006.

Building a government

Iraq's economy had been severely damaged by international sanctions imposed on Iraq after 1991's Persian Gulf War. Once the Hussein government was gone, the little economic production that still existed ceased. The conflicts between Shi'a and Sunnis and between religious fundamentalists and secularists grew worse as the economy of Iraq collapsed. With no jobs and few basic services such as electricity, some Iraqis turned to the insurgent (rebel) groups that fought against the temporary Iraqi government and the U.S. troops in Iraq. The insurgents carried out frequent bombings and suicide attacks, many of which targeted the U.S. military or Iraqis who were working with the Americans.

Putting together an Iraqi government that represented the Shi'a, the Sunnis, and the Kurds was extremely difficult. The interests of the three groups were at odds; resentments lingered from Hussein's reign. During a two-year period of squabbling among political leaders, the suicide bombings escalated. Finally, in 2005 the Iraqis held a democratic election, approved a constitution, and elected a government. The United Iraqi Alliance, a Shi'a-dominated coalition of groups backed by a highly influential religious and political leader, the Iranian Grand Ayatollah Ali al-Sistani (1930–), won about half of the votes.

The new government was stationed in the Green Zone of Iraq, the heavily gated and guarded headquarters of the coalition troops in Baghdad. Movement outside the Green Zone became increasingly dangerous. Many Iraqi and American observers noted that the new Iraqi government had little influence in Iraq outside the boundaries of the Green Zone.

In February 2006, the Askariya shrine in Samarra, considered to be the holiest Shi'a temple in Iraq, was bombed. The Shi'a assumed that Sunnis had done the bombing and angrily took to the streets seeking revenge. Within weeks, the U.S. media began to call the war in Iraq a civil war, but the Bush administration resisted that terminology.

A controversial war

Opponents of the Iraq war argued that the Bush administration had long wanted to invade Iraq, and thus had forced intelligence agencies to support their war with false reports of weapons of mass destruction and terrorist connections. Because the United States had begun the war without a clear mandate from the United Nations, some opponents claimed from the start that the war was illegitimate and perhaps illegal under international law.

After it was clear that there was little or no threat from weapons of mass destruction or al-Qaeda links in pre-invasion Iraq, supporters of the war argued that Saddam Hussein's regime had to be overthrown in order to protect the people of Iraq from their own leader. In addition, the Bush administration argued that the war was a central part of the war on terrorism, and that it was better to fight the terrorists in Iraq than in the United States. Despite some strong antiwar sentiments, support for the war among U.S. citizens remained relatively high for the first two years of fighting—long enough to see Bush win reelection in 2004. However, by 2006, the majority of Americans felt the administration had made a mistake in going to war and had handled the war badly. This public opinion led to the election of Democratic majorities in both houses of Congress.

By mid-October 2007, according to a Cable News Network (CNN) report, coalition deaths in the Iraqi war were as follows: 3,834 Americans, two Australians, 171 Britons, 13 Bulgarians, 1 Czech, 7 Danes, 2 Dutch, 2 Estonians, 1 Fijian, 1 Hungarian, 33 Italians, 1 Kazakh, 1 Korean, 3 Latvians, 21 Poles, 2 Romanians, 5 Salvadorans, 4 Slovaks, 11 Spaniards, 2 Thais, and 18 Ukrainians. About 28,276 U.S. soldiers have been wounded; many of them have lost limbs or received serious brain injuries. Cases of post-traumatic stress, a severe emotional disorder that results from having been in terrifying situations, are very high among the troops.

Figures on Iraqi deaths are less certain. According to the Iraq Body Count project team, there had been between 66,807 and 73,120 Iraqi civilian deaths by the end of June 2007. However, the *Lancet* medical journal estimated that by October 2006, 654,965 Iraqi civilians had been killed in the war, a figure disputed by the Iraq and U.S. governments and by the United Nations.

The surge

With most Americans hoping for a withdrawal of U.S. troops from Iraq, in January 2007 President Bush announced a new military strategy—a troop surge sending another twenty thousand U.S. troops to Iraq to fight the sectarian violence and promote security, particularly in Baghdad, starting in February 2007. With more troops in some areas, there were some small areas of peace in the war-torn country. Although protest against the war remained high, at the end of 2007 there were no plans for a U.S. withdrawal.

Irish Immigration

Nearly two million Irish people came to the United States from Ireland in the 1840s. Most of them crossed the ocean to escape the potato famine. Potatoes were the main crop grown by farmers in Ireland, and a fungus infestation devastated crops nationwide in 1845. Families sold everything they owned for money, and it still was not enough. Many starved.

As the Irish immigrants found steady work that allowed them to save money, they sent for friends and relatives. This kept a continuous flow of Irish coming into America. In total, about 3.5 million Irish from

Ireland immigrated to the United States between 1820 and 1880. In the years between 1820 and 1860, the Irish accounted for one-third of all immigrants to America. Many more Irish emigrated from Britain, but because Britain was the point of departure, they were counted as British, not Irish, in immigration records.

Though not the poorest in Irish society, those who came to the United States were incredibly poor by American standards. Many of them did not have money beyond the ship fare, so they settled near the port at which they arrived. The main port of entry was **Ellis Island**, near New York City. New York City eventually was home to more Irishmen than Dublin, Ireland.

An 1870 census (a periodic count of the population) revealed that the Irish comprised 14.5 percent of the populations of large American cities. They dominated the population in New England and accounted for 22 percent of **New York**'s population that year. They and the Germans made up the largest immigrant group in 1870.

Labor

Irish immigrants were laborers who took dangerous jobs that no one else wanted. The men worked the coal mines and built railroads and canals while the women worked as domestic (household) help. American businesses wasted no time in taking advantage of the cheap labor supplied by the Irish. Companies threatened to replace uncooperative employees with cheap Irish workers; this led to more tension between the Irish and the rest of the population.

Because of the tension between the Irish and everyone else, finding jobs became increasingly difficult for Irish immigrants. It was not uncommon for storefront windows to boldly feature handwritten signs that read "NINA" (No Irish Need Apply).

Second- and third-generation Irish immigrants (children and grandchildren of those who had sailed to America) often took jobs as police officers, firefighters, and schoolteachers. These generations achieved higher levels of education, which allowed them to earn more money.

Religion

The Irish were disliked by nearly every other ethnic group, and also by native-born Americans, because of their poor living conditions, their willingness to work for low wages, and their religion. Protestants (Christians who are not Catholics) and Catholics had a long history of conflict based on varying beliefs and an unwillingness to tolerate one another. The Irish were Catholic. In America, most Catholics were members of upper-class society. They were not accustomed to having to include or accept members of the lower class. The tension created by these class differences was an obstacle not easily overcome.

Protestant Americans watched as millions of Catholics flooded their shores. Catholic churches were appearing on every street corner in some neighborhoods. It seemed to some as though Protestant neighborhoods were being overrun with Catholics. These Irish Catholics brought with them foreign customs and rituals that Americans and other ethnic groups did not understand. Conflict was virtually unavoidable. The Irish became the target of violence in big cities throughout the Northeast. Catholic churches were burned, and riots broke out.

Getting by

Persecution was not new to the Irish. Ireland was under British rule, so most Irish immigrants had never known freedom as Americans understood it. In their homeland, the Irish were controlled politically, economically, and religiously. They often formed secret organizations, usually with the help of their village priest, to meet their educational and economic needs. These societies allowed the Irish to form a strong identity. They stuck together for the sake of survival. This experience helped them as immigrants in America as well.

The Irish were excellent organizers. They recognized the value of teamwork, and their ability allowed them to break into the American political system. Since most of them lived in big cities, they were able to take control of politics like no other ethnic group had ever done. The Irish put the power into the hands of the working class and established loyalty among that large voting group. They formed political machines (organized political groups that ensure the loyalty of voters by repaying them for their votes with favors such as money, jobs, or gifts) that took over major American cities from the mid-eighteenth into the twentieth century. Although political machines were considered unethical, they allowed the Irish to survive in a hostile environment.

Iroquois Confederacy

The Iroquois Confederacy was a political and social alliance of five Indian tribes (later six) who lived in the northeastern part of North America. The Iroquois are also known as Haudenosaunee, meaning "people of the longhouse." The nations that were members of the confederacy were the Cayuga, Mohawk, Oneida, Onondaga, and Seneca, and later the Tuscarora. Long before Europeans arrived on the continent, the Iroquois had formed a complex, democratic society. In fact, some historians consider the Iroquois Confederacy one of the world's oldest democracies.

The dark times

The story of the founding of the Iroquois Confederacy is known today through oral, or spoken, history, handed down from generation to generation of the Iroquois people. The story probably blends people and events from the Iroquois past and it does not provide dates, but most historians accept it as a very useful outline of Iroquois history.

Some time before European contact, the Mohawk, Onondaga, Seneca, Cayuga, and Oneida nations engaged in near-constant warfare. The darkest times were during the reign of a warlike Onondaga chief named Todadaho, who was feared far and wide. Many accounts describe him as a cannibal, and in fact, in some native northeastern cultures people believed that eating their victims in battle gave warriors better fighting skills.

Into this violent era entered the prophet Deganawida, a member of either the Huron or the Mohawk tribe. Deganawida grieved to see so much war and conflict in the world around him, and he traveled far from home seeking solutions. In his travels, he met Hiawatha, who was a Mohawk or Onondaga and told him of his hopes for peace and good government. Deganawida believed that the creator of all things had given humans the power to reason, and that by using clear thinking they could find the path to a balanced, peaceful society. Hiawatha was captivated by Deganawida's words and offered to serve as his orator (someone who makes public speeches). Together they traveled to a Mohawk village to begin teaching people the rules for a peaceful society.

Deganawida eventually won the Mohawks over and went on to convince the Oneida, Seneca, and Cayuga nations to join the Mohawks in a

Members of the six-nation Iroquois Confederacy in front of the General Assembly Building at the United Nations headquarters. The Iroquois Confederacy was a political and social alliance of five (later six) northeastern Indian tribes. AP IMAGES

union of tribes. Using nonviolent and respectful persuasion, Deganawida was finally able to convince even Todadaho to give up his constant fighting and join the union. Deganawida then planted the Tree of Peace as a symbol of the confederacy at the Onondaga Nation near present-day Syracuse, **New York**. The confederacy called itself the Haudenosaunee, or people of the longhouse, because they pledged to live peacefully under one government, in the same way several families might live together as distinct units under the protection of one roof. Some historians date the union around 1100 BCE, though others believe it happened later in history, sometime between 1350 and 1550 CE.

The rules of the confederacy

The Iroquois nations created an oral constitution called the Great Law. Under its rules of government, the Grand Council of Chiefs, made up of forty-nine chiefs from the five tribes, led the confederacy. The Grand Council gathered at Onondaga to establish laws and customs and to guide the interaction of the members of the confederacy. Each tribe had an equal voice in the council, and the system was mostly democratic. Iroquois women played a major role in decision making. Deganawida, who came to be known as the Great Peacemaker, is credited with creating the advanced political system. As the council developed over the years, it tried to negotiate among peoples, whether in relations between tribes or in treaties with European settlers arriving on its lands.

When the American colonies were established in the Northeast, the united Iroquois nations presented a strong front to avoid invasion of their lands. One of the Iroquois' strengths was their willingness to include new members within the confederacy, such as the Tuscarora nation of **North Carolina** and members of the Huron tribe. By 1677, the confederacy was one of the most powerful groups of North American Indians, consisting of approximately sixteen thousand people. It stretched over a large area of what is now New York State and beyond.

Influencing the founding fathers

In the eighteenth century, the American colonists were eager to form their own democracy. Impressed by the democratic Iroquois Confederacy, they sought the advice of the Iroquois when preparing the Albany Plan of Union of 1755, an attempt to unite the original American **thirteen colonies** under one federal government as the Iroquois had united its nations. In 1787, founders of the new nation, **Thomas Jefferson** (1743–1826), **John Adams** (1735–1826), and John Hancock (1737–1793) were all inspired by the Great Law of the Iroquois Confederacy as they debated the writing of the U.S. **Constitution**.

The Iroquois became divided during the **American Revolution**, the colonists' war of independence from England (1775–83). Some Iroquois groups fought on the side of the colonists and others fought with England. Before the war was even over, the new U.S. government allowed land companies to buy up most of the Iroquois lands. The internal division weakened the once-strong Iroquois union, and the confederacy began to fall apart. Many Iroquois groups, particularly those who had fought with the British, left for Canada, never to return. The Iroquois who remained held onto as much land as they could. Today, their descendants own eight reservations in New York and **Wisconsin**. The Iroquois Confederacy was the country's eleventh-largest Native American group in the year 2000, according to the U.S. census.

Isolationism

Isolationism is a policy of nonparticipation in international economic and political relations. It was practiced by the United States from the end of the presidency of **George Washington** (1732–1799; served 1789–97) through the first half of the twentieth century, though not steadily.

This policy of abstaining from foreign relations is what kept the United States from entering into **World War I** (1914–18) until 1917. Only reluctantly did President **Woodrow Wilson** (1856–1924; served 1913–21) seek Congress's permission to enter the war. The U.S. economy had recently changed from mostly agricultural to mostly industrial, and this shift made the nation partly dependent on international trade. This new situation made it difficult for the United States to continue with its isolationism.

Most Americans felt that World War I was Europe's war, and the majority greatly resented the loss of American lives for a cause they could not embrace. Although they supported their soldiers overseas during the war, when it was over the United States returned to an isolationist attitude.

The nation focused on internal affairs rather than international relations throughout the 1920s. The next decade brought the **Great Depression** (1929–41), and Americans were focused on daily survival. As the decade closed and Germany's Nazi Party leader Adolf Hitler (1889–1945) forced the beginning of **World War II** (1939–45), President **Franklin D. Roosevelt** (1882–1945; served 1933–45) insisted that the United States would remain neutral.

Despite this commitment to isolationism, it was Europe's need for American products and goods throughout the war that brought the United States out of its economic misery. Many Americans believed that staying out of the war would bring them both prosperity and peace, but Roosevelt's administration grew to favor intervention. The president's advisers warned him that isolationism would allow Germany to take control of Europe and Japan to dominate Asia, which would close major markets to American trade forever. When word of the atrocities of the Holocaust reached Roosevelt, he decided that the combination of economic and moral issues warranted a break from isolationism. Still, it was the Japanese bombing of **Pearl Harbor** on December 7, 1941, that shocked America out of its inaction and thrust it into World War II.

Italian and Greek Immigration

During the period from 1880 to 1920, millions of people in a huge wave of immigration came to the United States from southern and eastern Europe, including Italy and Greece. An estimated four million Italian immigrants arrived in the United States, making Italians the single largest European national group to move to America in that era. Great numbers of young Greek men were also part of this immigration wave. In fact, by 1925 one out of every four Greek men between the ages of fifteen and forty-five had gone to the United States.

Italian immigration

Italy experienced political turmoil and economic crisis at the end of the nineteenth century. Finding it difficult to support their families, many Italians decided to emigrate. Two of Italy's poorest regions, the island of Sicily and the region around Naples, accounted for over half the Italians who left their homes for the United States.

The United States attracted many Italians because it desperately needed workers. The American **Civil War** (1861–65) had killed over six hundred thousand young men, creating a labor shortage just when the country was building its major cross-country railroads and establishing factories and industrial centers. Young Italian men sought steady wages they could send home to their families. They left their homeland planning to return to Italy when economic circumstances improved. In fact, many Italians did return home after working in the United States for a short period.

Life for Italian Americans

Italian immigrants were among the poorest people to come to the United States in this period. They tended to take work as laborers in the cities of the northeastern United States, especially New York City and Boston, **Massachusetts**. Most immigrants from southern Italy could not read or write, and few spoke English. Thus, they were often forced to work in the lowest-paying jobs that no one else wanted.

Newly arrived Italian men used an employment system that revolved around a *padrone,* which means "boss." The padrone acted as a professional labor broker. Employers came to him to find workers, and job seekers came to him to find work. The padrone system contributed to a

Italian immigrants often moved to towns in America where people from their own region of Italy had settled. One of the most famous was Little Italy in New York, which had several Italian storefronts. AP IMAGES

concentration of Italian workers in certain industries such as construction, where the padrones had contacts.

When they arrived in the United States, it was common for Italian Americans to move into a neighborhood where people from their own town or region of Italy had settled. Several families from the same Italian town often lived next to each other on the same street in Boston or New York, maintaining the same social ties they had in Italy. As these neighborhoods grew, they each became known as Little Italy.

Sometime around **World War I** (1914–18), prejudice against Italians became strong. Non-Italian Americans resented that the Italian

Americans retained their language and culture and lived in tight-knit groups. They were suspicious of their Catholic religion, and they looked down upon the poorer Italians who were forced to take low-paying jobs. Hostility against Italians began to decline in the 1930s.

Greek immigrants

The first Greek immigrants were farmers who suffered from poverty in an unstable Greek economy in the late nineteenth century. Most who decided to emigrate were uneducated, and many wished to come only long enough to earn money to send to their families.

Like the Italians, the Greek immigrants had a padrone system. Greek padrones, though, recruited workers directly from Greece to come to the United States under contract. As with the **indentured servitude** system of earlier times, the employers would pay for the workers' passage to America. In return, the worker would agree to work for a number of years at an agreed-upon (but always very low) wage. Many Greek families who could not otherwise make ends meet sent their sons to the United States under such contracts. Young men and boys under the padrone system often worked as shoe shine boys or as helpers to shopkeepers.

Between 1900 and 1920, about 350,000 Greek immigrants arrived in the United States. The majority tended to settle in the cities of the Northeast and Midwest, such as Boston, New York, and Chicago, **Illinois**. Many Greek immigrants eventually opened their own businesses. Once a Greek man had established a business in the United States, he often sent for a wife from his home village through an arranged marriage; the chosen woman would then immigrate to the United States.

Greek Americans suffered discrimination at first, and at times it was violent. But on the whole, they were treated somewhat better than the Italians and other southern Europeans arriving at the time.

Immigration Act of 1924

By the 1920s, prejudices against newly arrived immigrants resulted in anti-immigrant policies in the United States. Congress passed the Emergency Quota Act of 1921, which restricted the number of immigrants who could come into the United States based on people's nationality. Three years later, Congress passed the Immigration Act of 1924, making national quotas permanent. It radically reduced the maximum number of immigrants from any single country to a number equal to 2 percent of the number of that particular nationality that had resided in the United States in 1890—before the many Italians and Greeks had arrived.

The intent of the law was to preserve the United States as a country dominated by people with northern European, Protestant ancestors. The result of the law was to end forty years of mass migration from southern and eastern Europe.

J

Andrew Jackson

Andrew Jackson rose from humble backcountry origins to become a famous military hero and the seventh president of the United States. Many Americans, especially those of the western frontier, honored him as an example of the new, self-made American. Others viewed him as a military leader who used unnecessary brutality and as a president who exceeded his authority and divided his political party.

Youth during the American Revolution

Jackson's parents emigrated to the backwoods of **South Carolina** from northern Ireland in 1765, and Andrew's father died a few days before his birth. Jackson, who was born on March 15, 1767, was a reckless and quick-tempered boy. He attended some local schools, and could read and write, but he was less educated than any of the U.S. presidents before him.

The **American Revolution** (1775–83; the war for independence from Great Britain) overshadowed Jackson's youth. In 1779, the thirteen-year-old Andrew and his brother enlisted in the army and were soon captured by the British. During their captivity, both brothers caught smallpox, an infectious disease. The British released them, and they walked 40 miles home, barefoot and coatless. Two days after they arrived, Andrew's brother died. His mother died soon after. At fourteen, Jackson was alone. The hatred he felt for the British remained with him for life.

Controversial figure Andrew Jackson was a military leader and later the seventh president of the United States. THE LIBRARY OF CONGRESS

A young lawyer

After a somewhat wild youth, Jackson decided to study law. Admitted to the bar (licensed to practice law) in 1787, he set out for **Tennessee** to serve as a prosecuting attorney. He was soon appointed attorney general. Financial successes allowed him to begin building a plantation and to purchase slaves to work on it. He served in the Tennessee state legislature, then briefly as a U.S. senator, and later served six years as a judge in the Tennessee Superior Court.

Jackson married a divorced woman, Rachel Donelson Robard, in 1794, and was a devoted husband. In 1806, a man insulted Rachel's honor. Jackson challenged him to a duel and killed him.

Military career

Jackson began his military career as commander of a group of Tennessee volunteers in the **War of 1812** (a conflict between England and the United States over trade issues). In this role, he destroyed a large part of the population of the Creek Indians in **Mississippi** Territory who had been involved in skirmishes with U.S. troops. Promoted into the regular army, Jackson led a large force against the British at the Battle of New Orleans in 1815. He triumphed in the battle and emerged as the war's greatest hero.

Three years later, Jackson invaded **Florida**, which at the time was a Spanish territory, in pursuit of Seminole Indians resisting relocation to **Indian Territory** (present-day **Oklahoma**). Thus began the first of the **Seminole Wars** (1817–18). Many of Jackson's actions in Florida were questionable. He ordered the execution of two British subjects suspected of aiding the Indians, and his brutal conduct toward Indians earned him a reputation among journalists and politicians as a tyrant and a murderer. But after his campaign, Spain ceded Florida to the United States, which greatly pleased many Americans. Jackson's popularity as a no-nonsense military leader grew.

For a short period in 1821, Jackson served as governor of the Florida Territory. He resigned when the Tennessee legislature chose him for the

U.S. Senate. Two years later, he stepped down to make his first bid for the presidency.

Lost election of 1824

In the 1824 election, different factions of the **Democratic-Republican Party** ran for president. Jackson won the highest number of popular and electoral votes (votes cast by the **electoral college**, made up of members chosen by each state to elect a president), but he did not have the majority of electoral votes required by the **Constitution**. Therefore, it was up to the House of Representatives to select a president. When it chose **John Quincy Adams** (1767–1848; served 1825–29), Jackson was convinced that the election had been fixed. For the next four years, Jackson's supporters made things difficult for the Adams administration, opposing many of its initiatives.

Jackson ran for president again in 1828. In this campaign, his supporters emerged as the new "Jacksonian" **Democratic Party**. Supporters of Adams were called National Republicans, later to become the **Whig Party**. Jackson won an overwhelming victory.

The presidency

Jackson's first term was marked by a conflict between him and his vice president, **John C. Calhoun** (1782–1850) over the issue of nullification, which held that if a state objects to a federal law, it has the right to block the law's enforcement. (See **Nullification Controversy**.) Calhoun's home state of South Carolina attempted to nullify the tariffs (taxes on imports and exports) of 1828 and 1829; Jackson reacted by calling for military action against South Carolina. It took a compromise tariff to avoid confrontation.

As president, Jackson continued to try to take Indian land, as he had done in the military. He promoted the Indian Removal Act, which was passed by Congress in 1830. The act called for the forced march of thousands of American Indians from their native lands in the Southeast along the **"Trail of Tears"** into Indian Territory, causing great suffering and death.

Jackson's second term as president was dominated by his campaign to abolish the national bank system, which he felt gave too much power to the federal government and favored the Northeast over the South and

West. He forced the removal of federal deposits from the Second Bank of the United States and distributed them among a favored group of state banks. Senate members protested, declaring the president's actions unconstitutional, but he would not budge on the issue. In his last months in office, a national financial crisis resulted from these drastic measures. His critics began to call him "King Andrew," because they believed he had taken more power than the Constitution allowed a president.

After his presidency, Jackson retired to his estate in Tennessee, the Hermitage, but remained a powerful force in the Democratic Party. He died in 1845.

Jamestown, Virginia

In 1606, King James I (1566–1625) of England granted a charter to the Virginia Company of London, giving it rights to establish a business in the New World under the protection of the English. The one charter gave two companies, the Plymouth Company and the London Company, shares in land between the Cape Fear River of North Carolina and Bangor, **Maine**. The northern part of this land grant went to the Plymouth Company, and the southern part went to the London Company.

On December 20, 1606, the Virginia Company sent three ships, the *Susan Constant*, the *Godspeed*, and the *Discovery*, to the Chesapeake Bay region for the London Company. On May 24, 1607, the passengers disembarked and called the site for their settlement Jamestown, after King James I. Through persistence and determination, the settlers made Jamestown the first permanent English settlement in America.

Challenges

The settlement faced difficulties from its very first moments. It was to be governed by a local council of seven men. The men who were chosen to serve on the council, however, hated and feared each other. Many of the settlers were headstrong adventurers with individual ambitions. Others were unwilling to put in the work needed to establish a viable community, choosing to relax and play games instead of growing food and working. Disease weakened and killed many of the settlers in the first year.

This fort was built by the first English settlers on their arrival to Jamestown, Virginia, in 1607. AP IMAGES

Only after three council members returned to England and three others died did the settlement get effective leadership, under Captain **John Smith** (c. 1580–1631). In 1608, Smith took firm control of the settlement. Four to six hours of work were required from each person every day. Smith also worked to improve relationships with the native Indians, though this was not an easy task. In 1609, Smith was injured and returned to England.

A new charter was written that year, and the seven-man council was replaced by a governor. The Virginia Company sent several hundred settlers to strengthen the colony before the governor's arrival, but their own arrival strained the settlement's resources. Without a strong leader like Smith, most of the settlers died during the Jamestown winter of 1609 to 1610, which is called the "starving time." Of the 490 settlers Smith had left behind, only sixty survived the food shortages, disease, and Indian attacks of the winter.

New beginnings

In 1610, the new governor arrived and imposed a strict government. With additional supplies, increased manpower, and required work, the colonists began to be successful. In 1614, the colony switched from exporting ship masts and lumber to exporting **tobacco**. The economic outlook of the colony brightened somewhat.

In time, disease, violent clashes with Indians, and difficulty with laborers undermined the potential success of the tobacco crops. In 1619, the company reorganized again, sending another 1,216 people to Jamestown. The company authorized the colonists to form the **House of Burgesses**, the first representative elected assembly in America. But these efforts failed to bring the necessary profits for the company's survival, and King James I dissolved the bankrupt Virginia Company in 1624. This made **Virginia** the first royal colony, controlled directly by the king's ministers rather than through a company.

Decline

By 1625, 124 people resided in Jamestown, but more and more settlers began to move to the countryside to support their tobacco farms. In spite of efforts to revive its importance, Jamestown was badly located on swampy ground, and when fires in 1676 and 1698 destroyed the town, the government of Virginia was moved further inland to Williamsburg in 1699.

Only a few excavated foundations and the ruined tower of the brick church remain on the site of Jamestown today. The United States declared Jamestown a national historic site in 1940, and the Colonial National Historical Park welcomes visitors to it.

Japanese Immigration
See **Asian Immigration**

Japanese Internment Camps

The Japanese attack on the U.S. military base at Pearl Harbor, **Hawaii**, on December 7, 1941, surprised and outraged Americans. The **Pearl Harbor attack** heightened long-standing anti-Asian sentiment among many Americans living along the western coast of the United States, and

Manzanar War Relocation Center was a Japanese internment camp during World War II. Approximately 110,000 people were forcibly relocated to Japanese internment camps. THE LIBRARY OF CONGRESS

the hostility toward Americans of Japanese descent culminated in the forced removal of approximately 110,000 people to Japanese internment (prison) camps.

Evolution of an executive order

Many Americans were convinced that Japanese Americans in Hawaii assisted the Japanese in their attack on Pearl Harbor. After the attack, nearly fifteen hundred Japanese suspected of disloyal actions were rounded up. Those not regarded as immediate security risks were restricted from traveling without permission, barred from areas near strategic installations, and forbidden to possess arms, short-wave radios, and maps.

Fear that Japanese living on American soil would support Japan's war effort fueled a desire to remove Japanese and Japanese American residents altogether. Military leaders, patriotic groups, newspapers, and politicians joined in calls for action. They warned about the potential for sabotage by the issei (first-generation, Japanese-born immigrants) and nisei (second-generation, U.S.-born citizens) in America.

The anxiety reached such a feverish pitch that President **Franklin D. Roosevelt** issued Executive Order 9066 on February 19, 1942. The order authorized the military to designate "military areas" from which "any or all persons may be excluded." Under this order, the military was able to force evacuations of issei and nisei throughout the West Coast. In March 1942, the War Relocation Authority was created to administer relocation centers.

Evacuation

At first, the military called upon the Japanese Americans living in the western parts of **California**, **Oregon**, and **Washington**, and along the **Arizona**-Mexico border, to leave voluntarily for the interior of the country. But the interior communities refused to accept the newcomers, and the military had to issue a freeze order requiring Japanese Americans to remain where they were. Then between March and June 1942, the military ordered them to leave their homes to report to temporary assembly centers.

The evacuees were given at most ten days, though sometimes as few as two days, to sell, discard, or store their belongings. Many Americans took advantage of the evacuees' unfortunate circumstances, buying their furniture, houses, and automobiles for low prices. Some Japanese Americans managed to store their belongings in churches or community buildings, but many of these were looted during the war. Evacuees were allowed to bring to the relocation camps only what they could carry.

The War Relocation Authority (WRA) created ten permanent relocation camps in the interior. Each camp held between ten and eleven thousand people. A typical camp consisted of wooden barracks covered with tar paper, and each barrack was subdivided into one-room apartments. The apartments were furnished with army cots, blankets, and a light bulb. Families or unrelated groups of individuals were assigned to share each room, reducing privacy. Bathing, washing, and dining facilities were communal. The camps were surrounded by barbed wire and patrolled by armed military guards.

Impact

Camp life was difficult for the Japanese Americans. Evacuees were allowed to bring with them only the bare essentials of clothing, bedding, and eating utensils. This meant they suffered the loss of familiar possessions and comforts. The cramped quarters strained family relationships, and many parents complained that it was difficult to discipline their children. Social order within Japanese American communities was affected as the traditional powers enjoyed by elder males were challenged by the restraints of life within the camps. Traditional customs in their lives, such as arranged marriages, disintegrated.

Angered by the loss of their rights and freedom, and bitter towards the U.S. government, internees sometimes directed their hostilities toward each other. Riots broke out in some camps.

Actions by the WRA worsened things in the camp communities. In 1943, Japanese Americans were labeled as "loyal" or "disloyal." The disloyal residents were moved to a segregation center within one of the camps. In 1944, the army began drafting men from the camps to serve in **World War II** (1939–45), sparking a considerable resistance movement.

Dissolution

Throughout World War II, U.S. courts upheld the legality of internment, ruling that the military had the power to take precautionary action against Americans who shared an ethnic heritage with the enemy. In December 1944, the U.S. **Supreme Court** ruled to discontinue detention of citizens whose loyalty had been established. The decision was nearly pointless, however, as President Roosevelt had announced the termination of his executive order the day before the ruling.

The evacuees still in relocation centers were allowed to leave at will, but many stayed in the camps in fear of hostilities outside. In June 1945, the camps were officially scheduled for closure by the end of the year, and remaining residents were to be forced to leave, if necessary.

It was not until 1976 that the U.S. government acknowledged any wrongdoing in the affair. In that year, President **Gerald R. Ford** (1913–2006; served 1974–77) officially rescinded Executive Order 9066 and issued a formal apology to Japanese Americans.

In 1981, pressure from the Japanese American community led Congress to establish the Commission on Wartime Relocation and Internment of Civilians. The commission report concluded that the internment was not justified by military necessity and was instead motivated by prejudice, war hysteria, and a failure of political leadership. Federal courts vacated opinions that had upheld the constitutionality of the internment. In 1988, Congress passed a law issuing a formal apology and establishing a fund of $1.25 billion to pay compensation of $20,000 to each surviving internment victim.

Jay's Treaty

The United States and Great Britain signed Jay's Treaty on November 19, 1794. It was a follow-up to the **Treaty of Paris** of 1783, which was supposed to establish peaceful relations between the two countries after the **American Revolution** (1775–83). Jay's Treaty was meant to solve some persistent problems that were causing diplomatic tensions and threatening to provoke another war.

Growing pains

The United States had several complaints against Great Britain after the American Revolution. According to the Treaty of Paris, the English were supposed to abandon posts in the Northwest Territory near Canada. Britain not only refused to do so, but it also complicated American attempts to make peace with the region's Native American tribes.

At sea, Great Britain actively prevented U.S. ships from trading in British ports. British naval vessels regularly impressed, or kidnapped, U.S. seamen into British service, and this too was a constant strain on diplomatic relations.

Great Britain had its own complaints against the United States. British creditors with prewar debts in America were having difficulty collecting their debts in state courts, and British Loyalists were struggling to regain confiscated property in America. Disagreements about territorial boundaries also caused problems.

War

All of these issues were complicated by the outbreak of war between Great Britain and France in 1793. As a young country, the United States was unprepared to go to war on behalf of either country, but neutrality was difficult to maintain. U.S. treaties with France enabled French privateers to equip themselves and operate in U.S. ports. The United States also had promised to defend the French West Indies. Both the French and U.S. navies, however, were greatly inferior to the British. Great Britain and Spain were allies against France. Both countries had territories, and boundary disputes, along American borders. The United States could hardly risk conflict with Great Britain and Spain together.

American commercial interests also had to be protected. Great Britain was still the main trade partner for the United States. Great Britain provided many manufactured goods to the states and supplied credit. Though support for both the French and English existed in the United States, President **George Washington** (1732–99; served 1789–97) issued a proclamation of neutrality in April 1793.

The treaty

Attempts to remain neutral caused problems with both Great Britain and France. The British were particularly aggressive in challenging neutrality. Increased British **impressment** of U.S. sailors and the seizure of 250 U.S. ships in the French West Indies brought the countries to the brink of war. Washington sent John Jay (1745–1829), the chief justice of the U.S. **Supreme Court**, to England to negotiate a treaty.

Under Jay's Treaty, the English agreed to vacate the Northwest Territory, restore U.S. trading privileges in British ports and the East Indies, compensate for seized ships, and end discrimination of U.S. commerce. The United States opened the Mississippi River to the English, promised to pay debts owed to British merchants, and agreed to close U.S. ports to the outfitting of privateers for British enemies.

The treaty that Jay negotiated was unacceptable to many Americans and sparked sharp division among politicians and citizens. It provoked furious debate in Congress. Though it failed to resolve some of the most divisive issues, such as impressment of sailors and recognition of U.S. neutrality, the treaty did manage to stabilize diplomatic relations. Though disappointed, President Washington signed it, believing it to be the only alternative to war. Thanks to intense effort by his administration, it was passed by the Senate in February 1796.

Jay's Treaty had far-reaching implications. Most importantly, it avoided war between the United States and Great Britain during a vulnerable time of development for the young country. But it complicated U.S. relations with France, which considered the treaty a breach of its own agreements with the United States. An undeclared naval war between the two countries followed. Political debates among Americans further inspired the organization of the **Republican Party** and the party system in American politics.

Jazz

Jazz music in the United States has roots dating back to the arrival of the first African American slaves in North America. Originally, the blues sound was a combination of rhythms made by instruments brought from Africa, combined with the fiddle strains and songs from white settlers from the British Isles. This blend evolved until it emerged in the 1890s as a type of music called ragtime. Ragtime eventually became jazz.

New Orleans, **Louisiana**, is considered the birthplace of jazz. Most early residents of New Orleans were Creole, people of Spanish, French, or African descent, and the early musicians brought the sound of their particular heritage to create a genre of jazz that became known as Dixieland. Another term for this type of music, which was played on brass instruments, is creole jazz. Dixieland music is marching band music with offbeat rhythms and improvised solos. Early Dixieland musicians included pianist Ferdinand "Jelly Roll" Morton (1885–1941) and cornet player Joe "King" Oliver (1885–1938). Morton is considered to be the first jazz composer.

Leaders of the band

One of the most famous jazz musicians was Louis Armstrong (1901–1971). Armstrong was born in New Orleans and learned to play the cornet as a young teen. Throughout the 1920s, he performed in Chicago, **Illinois**, and New York City, eventually landing a long-term engagement at Connie's Inn, a popular and glamorous nightclub in New York City's Harlem. Armstrong became known for his ability to improvise. His career spanned decades and included performing on **Broadway** and singing. He is heralded as a key figure in the evolution of jazz music.

Often taking jazz in new directions was **Miles Davis** (1926–1991), a jazz trumpeter and composer. While never as technically talented as some of his contemporaries, Davis was influential in jazz circles for his style, which became known as cool jazz.

Another jazz great was **Duke Ellington** (1899–1974), who regularly performed at the Cotton Club, a music hot spot of the 1920s. Ellington played piano but was most influential as a composer and bandleader. Along with bandleader Fletcher Henderson (1898–1952), he created the Big Band sound, which features a jazz orchestra with more than one musician playing each instrument. Ellington's signature sound was one that incorporated mutes and growl techniques in the horns.

Thomas "Fats" Waller (1904–1943) was another jazz great who made a name for himself playing piano in Harlem nightclubs. Jazz was the premier genre of music throughout the 1920s, and its popularity knew no bounds. Paul Whiteman (1890–1967) was a bandleader who was promoted as the Jazz King. His most famous contribution to jazz was a 1924 concert that introduced the new song "Rhapsody in Blue," written by George Gershwin (1898–1937). George and his brother Ira (1896–1983) were the most successful songwriters of the Jazz Age, and their music combined elements from jazz, classical, and even opera. These crossover sounds found a strong fan base in white audiences.

Beyond the Jazz Age

As America entered the **Great Depression** (1929–41), jazz decreased in popularity. Its sound was simply too celebratory, and Americans were not in any mood to celebrate. Millions had lost their jobs and homes, and their daily lives were a struggle. The new music of choice was **folk music**, the lyrics of which reflected this new experience of loss and injustice.

There were a couple of exceptions. Ella Fitzgerald (1917–1996) enjoyed a long and illustrious career as a jazz singer. She began singing jazz with the orchestra of bandleader Chick Webb (1909–1939) in the mid-1930s. Before the end of the decade, she had recorded several hit songs and gained notoriety. Fitzgerald left the band in 1942 to embark on what would be a successful solo career. Benny Goodman (1909–1986) was another popular jazz musician whose clarinet style eventually fused into a type of music called swing. Goodman was one of only a few white jazz musicians who was able to build a career with his music.

Jazz had its loyal followers, however. Music of the 1940s included jazz, but its sounds were often incorporated and mixed with those of classical, blues, and swing. Jazz pianist William "Count" Basie (1904–1984) was also a bandleader whose band performed for more than fifty years. He incorporated jazz in a structured, orchestral setting and his band backed some of the most prominent jazz vocalists of the time, including Billie Holiday (1915–1959), Lester Young (1909–1959), and Herschel Evans (1909–1939). Pianist Thelonious Monk (1920–1982) made his first recordings in the mid-1940s and often collaborated with other jazz greats including saxophonist Sonny Rollins (1930–), saxophonist John Coltrane (1926–1967), Miles Davis, and Charlie Parker (1920–1955).

Charlie "Yardbird" Parker was a jazz saxophonist considered by historians to be one of the great jazz pioneers. Parker's sound eventually fused into a form of jazz called bebop. This form is characterized by fast tempos and improvisations that are based on harmony rather than melody. Parker's work in 1945 with trumpeter Dizzy Gillespie (1917–1993) took the jazz world by storm.

The first annual Newport Jazz Festival was established in July 1954. This was an act of courage on the part of socialites Elaine and Louis Lorillard. Among wealthy white crowds, jazz was considered inappropriate for the more sedate, proper country-club audiences. But six thousand jazz lovers paid up to $5 a ticket for the two-day **Rhode Island** program. Twenty-six thousand fans attended the 1955 Newport Jazz Festival and were entertained by two hundred musicians. The event moved to New York City in 1972 and became a two-site festival when it returned to Newport in 1981. Since 1986, it has been known as the JVC Jazz Festival.

The 1960s, like the 1930s, featured folk music, again, because its lyrics reflected the political and social unrest of the era. The 1970s were not notable for jazz music, either, although some musicians experimented with jazz-rock fusion. The early 1980s saw artists like Pat Metheny (1954–), Al Jarreau (1940–), George Benson (1943–), Chuck Mangione (1940–), and Kenny G (1956–) on the charts. Not one of

One of the great pioneers of jazz, saxophonist Charlie Parker helped influence the form of jazz called bebop.
HULTON ARCHIVE/GETTY IMAGES

these musicians was a jazz purist, but each mixed jazz sounds with other genres such as pop, rhythm and blues, and fusion. In an era of mixed sound, two names stood out in jazz circles. Trumpeter Wynton Marsalis (1961–) surprised the jazz world with his mastery of technique. By the time he was nineteen years old, Marsalis had signed a contract with a major recording label. Having studied classical music as a teen, Marsalis became the first musician ever to win Grammy Awards in both jazz and classical in the same year (1984).

Harry Connick Jr. (1967–) reached stardom at the age of twenty when he released his first recording in 1988. Connick's New Orleans–style piano playing and smooth vocals made him a favorite crossover artist whose music was played on jazz and pop music radio stations. Like his contemporary Marsalis, he had studied both classical and jazz; at one point, he had studied piano under the tutelage of Marsalis's father, Ellis.

Although jazz was not one of the more popular music genres of the 1990s and the first decade of the twenty-first century, it maintained a loyal following. Some new musicians arrived on the scene, most notably singer-pianist Diana Krall (1964–). In an era when musicians relied upon elaborate stage performances and music videos to enhance their acts and popularity, jazz musicians had difficulty competing.

Jazz Age
See **Jazz; Roaring Twenties**

Thomas Jefferson

Thomas Jefferson was the third president of the United States and the main author of the **Declaration of Independence** (1776). This important document declared America's original **thirteen colonies** independent of England and profoundly influenced the future of American politics. It also expressed Jefferson's lifelong beliefs in natural rights, equality, individual liberties, and self-government. Along with being one of the nation's founders (political leaders in the time of the **American Revolution** [1775–83] who created and signed the Declaration of Independence and/or the **Constitution**) and great politicians, Jefferson was renowned for accomplishments in a remarkable variety of fields.

Jefferson was born on April 13, 1743, at Shadwell, his father's plantation in central **Virginia**'s Albemarle County. Jefferson's father was a self-educated farmer who became a legislator in the Virginia **House of Burgesses**, the legislative body of Virginia's colonial government under Great Britain. Jefferson's mother was the daughter of a wealthy and socially prominent Virginia family that owned slaves. As a child, Jefferson loved horseback riding and music, but he was also very serious about his studies, and he had a love of learning that continued throughout his life.

A variety of influences

While at the College of William and Mary, in Williamsburg, Virginia, Jefferson studied foreign and classical languages, mathematics, and the natural sciences. He was captivated by the ideas of the Enlightenment, a philosophic movement of the time that focused on the great power of human reason to create a rational society of equal individuals. In 1762, Jefferson began studying law and then started a successful law practice. This put him in frequent contact with some of the leading men of Virginia, including **Patrick Henry** (1736–1799), a fiery advocate of revolution against Great Britain.

On January 1, 1772, Jefferson married Martha Wayles Skelton, the educated daughter of a wealthy Williamsburg, Virginia, lawyer. With the land and slaves they inherited from their fathers, the Jeffersons were one of the wealthiest families in Virginia, guaranteeing Jefferson a role in Virginia politics. The newlyweds moved into Monticello, a mansion Jefferson designed, near Charlottesville, Virginia.

Revolutionary political career

In 1769, Jefferson was elected to the Virginia House of Burgesses, where he served for six years. In 1774, Jefferson joined a group of legislators who opposed England's domination over Virginia. They prepared a resolution to support the **Boston Tea Party**, a protest against the British tax on tea. The British-appointed governor of Virginia reacted by dissolving the House, prompting its members to meet to form a new plan of action. Jefferson submitted a paper, *A Summary View of the Rights of British America,* presenting the concept of "natural rights"—that people have certain rights that transcend civil laws and that cannot be taken away—which Jefferson would more fully describe in the Declaration of Independence. In this paper, Jefferson also forcefully denied that the

British Parliament held political authority over the colonists, and he demanded free trade and an end to British taxation. The essay was very influential in the revolutionary movement, and Jefferson's fame spread.

Two years later, Jefferson was appointed to a committee to write the Declaration of Independence. Although debate continues to this day over the exact circumstances of its composition, most historians agree that Jefferson wrote the original draft of the document in June 1776 and that he then submitted it to two committee members, **John Adams** (1735–1826) and **Benjamin Franklin** (1706–1790), who suggested minor changes before sending it to the colonial congress. The delegates debated the text line by line for two and a half days, then adopted it on July 4, 1776.

American statesman

During the American Revolution, Jefferson served as a member of the Virginia legislature and then as the governor of Virginia. Following the death of his wife in 1782, Jefferson retired from public office and wrote his only published book, *Notes on the State of Virginia*. The book described the physical environment of Virginia and expressed Jefferson's belief that the new republic should remain a nation of independent farmers.

In 1783, Jefferson again served as a delegate to the **Continental Congress** (the first national government of the United States), where he wrote rules for the governing of a region called the Northwest Territory, which included present-day **Ohio**, **Michigan**, **Indiana**, **Illinois**, **Wisconsin**, and part of **Minnesota**. Adopted a few years later as the Northwest Ordinance of 1787, these rules banned **slavery** in the territory north of the Ohio River and established how new states were to be admitted to the Union.

Clashes with Alexander Hamilton

In 1785, Jefferson became minister to France, and he remained in this position long enough to

Thomas Jefferson was the third president of the United States and the main author of the Declaration of Independence in 1776. THE LIBRARY OF CONGRESS

President George Washington, right, meeting with Secretary of State Thomas Jefferson, seated left, and Secretary of the Treasury Alexander Hamilton. Jefferson and Hamilton often clashed on policy; Hamilton supporters became known as Federalists and those backing Jefferson were Democratic-Republicans.
HULTON ARCHIVE/GETTY
IMAGES

see the beginning of the French Revolution in 1789. While he was in France, the U.S. Constitution was written. When he returned to the United States, he was appointed secretary of state by President **George Washington** (1732–1799; served 1789–97). A series of conflicts soon developed between Jefferson and the secretary of the treasury, **Alexander Hamilton** (1755–1804). Jefferson believed that the federal government should limit itself mainly to foreign affairs and allow states and local governments, led by farmers and workers, to handle local matters. Hamilton believed in a strong central government under the control of wealthy merchants and property owners. Their debate caused two groups to form: The backers of Hamilton became members of the **Federalist Party**, or Federalists, and those who supported Jefferson became part of the **Democratic-Republican Party**.

The Washington administration adopted Hamilton's ideas, and in 1793 Jefferson resigned. He ran for the presidency three years later, narrowly losing to his friend, incumbent vice president John Adams. At that time, the second-place finisher became vice president. Jefferson accepted the position, but he disagreed with Adams, who was a Federalist, over many issues. This was especially true with the passage of the **Alien and Sedition Acts** of 1798. These acts restricted the voting rights of recent immigrants and interfered with newspapers that criticized the government. Jefferson thought this seriously limited the freedoms of speech and the press and was contrary to the Constitution. Throughout his long political career, Jefferson never stopped being a champion of freedom and liberty.

Becomes third U.S. president

Jefferson defeated Adams in the election of 1800—the first election in which American voters were given a clear-cut choice between political parties. Jefferson served two terms as president, during which he cut government spending and simplified the way government was run. But his major achievement was the **Louisiana Purchase** in 1803, in which his administration bought a vast territory from France for $15 million, nearly doubling the size of the United States.

The question of slavery

Jefferson's personal life did not always seem to agree with his political philosophy, especially in regard to slavery. Though he owned about two hundred slaves, his personal and public papers reveal that he opposed the institution. He supported legislation to restrict slavery, but he stopped short of actions that might endanger his political support among slave owners. A rumor arose during Jefferson's first term as president that he had had a sexual relationship with his slave Sally Hemings (1773–1836) and had fathered several children with her. This story has persisted to the present day. Scientific testing has shown that descendants of Hemings may have also been Jefferson's descendants, but the facts probably will never be known for certain.

Jefferson retired to Monticello in 1809, having been in politics almost continuously for forty years. He turned his attention to architecture, farming, and education. In 1819, he designed and founded the University of Virginia, even selecting its faculty and planning its curriculum. During this time, Jefferson renewed his friendship with John Adams, with whom he had feuded for several years. Both men died on July 4, 1826, exactly fifty years after signing the Declaration of Independence.

Jefferson Memorial

In 1928, **Franklin D. Roosevelt** (1882–1945), then assistant secretary of the U.S. **Navy**, visited **Washington, D.C.**, and was disappointed that there was no memorial dedicated to President **Thomas Jefferson** (1743–1826; served 1801–9). Later, as president, Roosevelt expressed his view that such a memorial should be built, and in 1934 Congress passed a Joint Resolution to establish a Thomas Jefferson Memorial Commission (TJMC). The commission was given authority to plan, design, and construct the memorial.

The commission chose architect John Russell Pope (1874–1937) to submit a design. The National Competitions Committee for Architecture protested that the commission had not held a design contest, a more democratic selection process that Jefferson himself would have desired. Conflict notwithstanding, Pope designed a memorial based

The Jefferson Memorial in Washington D.C., was completed in 1943. SAUL LOEB/AFP/GETTY IMAGES

on the Pantheon in Rome, which Jefferson had publicly declared to be a perfect model of a circular building. An adaptation of the design, favored by the Commission of Fine Arts, was accepted in 1936. Pope's death the following year led to further controversy as to which design was better, Pope's original, or the modified version. Ultimately, the TJMC chose one of Pope's earlier Pantheon designs and then had it modified by Pope's former associates. President Roosevelt approved it.

The memorial, which sits on the shore of the Potomac River Tidal Basin, directly south of the White House, was completed in 1943. It is constructed of marble and limestone and cost just over $3 million. In 1912, Japan gave the United States a gift of three thousand Japanese cherry trees, which line the Tidal Basin. Nearly four thousand more of these trees were planted in 1956.

Inside the monument stands a nineteen-foot bronze statue of Jefferson. Weighing in at 10,000 pounds, the statue was added four years after the official dedication of the memorial in 1943. Inside the statue chamber are inscribed quotations taken from the **Declaration of Independence** and personal letters from Jefferson to important figures from the early years of the United States.

Jewish Immigration

The first Jews to settle in North America came from two Dutch communities in 1654. One group was fleeing from Brazil, where the Portuguese had expelled a Dutch company called the **Dutch East India Company**. This group settled in New Netherland in the Dutch town of **New Amsterdam**, which became New York City when the English took it in 1664.

The second group included Jacob Barsimson, a Jew who sailed to New Amsterdam from the Dutch city of Amsterdam. More Jewish merchants followed from Amsterdam in 1655. By the time of the English conquest of New Netherland, around fifty Jews had lived in the colony, though not altogether as a community.

Built first synagogue

Many Jews migrated to New York City from 1690 to 1710. By 1692, they were meeting for worship in a private home, calling their congrega-

The first Jews to settle in North America came from two Dutch communities in 1654. Jewish immigration to the United States continued for centuries, including this group of young Jewish refugees immigrating during World War II in 1939. THE LIBRARY OF CONGRESS

tion Shearith Israel. In 1730, they received permission from authorities to build New York City's first synagogue. At the time of the **American Revolution** (1775–83), around four hundred Jews lived in the city.

A small community of Jews from the Caribbean settled in Newport, **Rhode Island**, in the middle of the seventeenth century, shortly after Jews settled in New Amsterdam. After New Amsterdam became New York, more Jews moved from there to Newport. By 1756, the Jewish community in Newport had both a synagogue and a school.

In the South, Jewish communities formed during the colonial period in Charleston, **South Carolina**, and Savannah, **Georgia**. Some fled from Savannah to Charleston in the 1740s for fear of Spanish invasions. Many returned to Savannah in the 1760s after the end of the **French and Indian War**.

Barred from public office

Around 1790, there were about fifteen hundred Jews in the United States. The year before, synagogues sent President **George Washington** (1732–1799; served 1789–97) notes of congratulation at his inauguration. They spoke of the importance of religious freedom, to which Washington responded that the United States "gives bigotry no sanction, to persecution no assistance." At the time, most states excluded non-Christians from serving in public office.

By 1820, the Jewish population in America had grown to around twenty-seven hundred. Their communities were concentrated in Newport; New York City; Philadelphia and Lancaster, **Pennsylvania**, Richmond, **Virginia**; Charleston; and Savannah. Philadelphia's first permanent synagogue was erected in 1782. Before the 1840s, there were no professionally trained rabbis in America. Congregations were led by a cantor, called the hazan.

Nineteenth and twentieth century immigration

During the nineteenth century, Jews began immigrating to North America in large numbers. The first immigrants came mainly from the German states (a group of nation-states in what is now Germany), which had begun to pass anti-Semitic laws (laws hostile to Jews) around 1830. Many of the new arrivals were rebels who had tried, and failed, to initiate a revolution against the German governments. The German immigrants were generally an elite group; many had been educated in the finest European universities and many were idealist and highly political. (See **German Immigration**.) With the new influx from the German states, the Jewish community in the United States grew to about 160,000 in 1860.

At the turn of the twentieth century, Jews from Eastern Europe began to arrive in large numbers. In fact, between 1881 and 1914, two million Eastern European Jews arrived in the United States. They came from lands that were considered part of Russia, but had once been part of Poland. The Russian government had discriminated against Jews, sending them to live in an agricultural region known as the Pale of Settlement, an area including Byelorussia, Latvia, Lithuania, Ukraine, and a part of Russia. The Pale became horribly overcrowded and its inhabitants lived in desperate poverty. From 1881 to 1906, they were subjected to pogroms, or state-sponsored violence by mobs. Many fled to other countries.

When they arrived in the United States, most Eastern European Jews were extremely poor and they differed greatly from the elite population of German Jews already in the country. They struggled to find their way in the new land, most frequently settling in large eastern cities like New York City; Chicago, **Illinois**; Boston, **Massachusetts**; and Philadelphia. They faced many difficulties. Adding to the toll of poverty, harsh working conditions, and difficulties adapting to a foreign culture, during the 1920s and 1930s anti-Semitism in the United States increased significantly.

World War II

When Nazi leader Adolf Hitler (1889–1945) rose to power in Germany in the early 1930s, Jews became the targets of persecution. By 1938, it had become clear to most Jews that Hitler and the Nazis intended to kill them all. Many tried to flee. When U.S. president **Franklin D. Roosevelt** (1882–1945; served 1933–45) learned of the violence against the Jewish people of Germany, he condemned Hitler's actions, but he did not alter the U.S. immigration laws to provide a way for the Jews to legally enter the country.

On May 13, 1939, over nine hundred people boarded the steamship *St. Louis* in Hamburg, Germany. Most were Jews fleeing the Nazis, and they had paid every penny they could beg or borrow to buy a place on the ship and to secure a landing permit for Cuba. But the Cuban government did not allow most of the passengers to disembark, breaking its own arrangements. The ship finally set sail for Florida, where the U.S. government turned the ship away saying the quota—the number of immigrants admitted to the country from Germany and Austria—had already been filled. The U.S. response was later called a "paper wall," erected to keep the imperiled Jews out of the United States. The passengers of the *St. Louis* were forced to sail back to Europe. Some found safety in other nations but many of the passengers would die at the hands of the Nazis.

During the years 1938 to 1941, about 110,000 Jews immigrated to the United States. Until the end of the war, the United States maintained its policy of not becoming involved in the rescue of European Jews.

Later immigration

Jews have continued to immigrate to the United States since World War II, especially from nations that were once part of the Soviet Union, where they faced violence and discrimination intermittently through history. In 2000, there were 6.15 million Jews in the United States, accounting for about 2 percent of the nation's population.

Jim Crow Laws

In 1877, as the **Reconstruction** era (1865–77), the period following the American **Civil War** (1861–65), drew to a close, the former **Confederate States of America** were freed from the control of the federal troops that had been stationed there to ensure the fair treatment of the freed slaves. With the troops gone, Southern whites began to assert policies of **segregation** (separation of blacks from whites in public places). Although the **Thirteenth Amendment**, **Fourteenth Amendment**, and **Fifteenth Amendment** to the U.S. **Constitution** had freed African Americans from **slavery** and declared them citizens with enforceable rights, white Southerners remained unwilling to share communities and facilities with African Americans as equals.

In 1875, Congress had passed a Civil Rights Act guaranteeing African Americans access to public facilities. When some minor efforts were made to enforce the act, southern state legislatures reacted by creating an entire legal system to separate the races in every aspect of daily life. The result was a web of public policies and practices—the "Jim Crow laws"—that relegated persons of color to second-class status.

Origin of the name

Thomas "Daddy" Rice, a white minstrel performer, popularized the phrase "Jim Crow" in 1828 when he created a stage character based on a slave named Jim owned by a Mr. Crow. Mocking African Americans through his presentation, Rice blackened his face with burnt cork ("blackface"), donned a ragged costume, shuffled as he danced, and sang "ev'ry time I turn around I jump Jim Crow." Rice's popular ditty, "Jump Jim Crow," became an integral part of his routine, and by the 1830s his act propelled blackface minstrelsy into American culture. Somehow, from its stage use, the term "Jim Crow" evolved to refer to the practice of racial segregation.

Plessy v. Ferguson

In the late nineteenth century, the U.S. **Supreme Court** made two decisions supporting the Jim Crow laws. In 1883, the Court struck down the 1875 Civil Rights Act, saying that it exceeded Congress's powers. In 1896, the Court ruled in *Plessy v. Ferguson* that racial segregation was legally acceptable.

In 1890, the state of **Louisiana** had passed a law requiring that "colored" and white persons be provided "separate but equal" railroad passenger car accommodations. In 1892, Homer Plessy (1863–1925), a person of one-eighth African American descent, refused to leave the "white" car on the East Louisiana Railroad. His case eventually ended up in the Supreme Court. The Court ruled that the state law providing for "separate but equal" facilities was a reasonable exercise of state police powers to promote the public good. In fact, the Court went further and held that separate facilities did not have to be identical.

The Jim Crow laws spread throughout the South, requiring the separation of the races in every facet of life, including transportation, schools, lodging, public parks, theaters, hospitals, neighborhoods, cemeteries, and restaurants. Interracial marriages were prohibited. Business owners and public institutions were prohibited from allowing African American and white customers to mingle. Though the law called for "separate but equal," facilities for African Americans were almost always inferior to those set up for whites.

Although the objective of Jim Crow laws was to eliminate any contact between blacks and whites as equals, the result was to deprive African Americans of key economic and social opportunities, adequate food, shelter, clothing, education, and health care. In addition, between 1890 and 1908, every state of the former Confederacy enacted laws to limit African American voting rights. With discriminatory voting requirements, African Americans (and many poor whites) were effectively barred from participation in the political arena.

Fighting Jim Crow

The **National Association for the Advancement of Colored People** (NAACP), created in 1909, took the lead in combating Jim Crow laws. It brought one lawsuit after another to the courts, disputing the constitutionality of Jim Crow. NAACP successes were few before **World War II** (1939–45). The turning point came in 1954 when the Supreme Court struck down public school segregation in the case *Brown v. Board of Education*. Reversing the earlier *Plessy* decision, the Court asserted that the separate but equal doctrine was unconstitutional in regard to public educational facilities.

The **civil rights movement** of 1954 to 1965 brought the injustice of Jim Crow in the South to the national attention. Although many white southerners resisted attempts to eliminate Jim Crow, civil rights activists kept up the pressure to end segregation until the federal government finally intervened. The Jim Crow era came to a close with a series of landmark federal laws passed by Congress during the 1960s. The most notable of the new federal laws were the **Civil Rights Act of 1964**, the **Voting Rights Act** of 1965, and the Fair Housing Act of 1968. The Jim Crow era had lasted from the 1880s to the 1960s. Its legacy was a society still struggling with the effects of "separate and unequal."

Andrew Johnson

Andrew Johnson became the seventeenth president of the United States on April 15, 1865, the morning that President **Abraham Lincoln** (1809–1865; served 1861–65) died. Johnson inherited the responsibility of helping the nation to reunite and redefine itself after the end of the American **Civil War** (1861–65). This period following the war, called **Reconstruction**, was challenging for the Democratic Johnson as tensions with the Republican Congress evolved. His stubbornness and aggressive tactics created battles with Congress that eventually led to the first impeachment of a U.S. president.

Early life

Andrew Johnson's rise to the presidency was remarkable for two reasons: He was the first person to attain the office without either legal or military training, and he managed to overcome the terrible poverty and dep-

Andrew Johnson became the seventeenth president of the United States on April 15, 1865, the morning that President Abraham Lincoln died. He spent his presidency trying to push forward Lincoln's Reconstruction policies. THE LIBRARY OF CONGRESS

rivation of his upbringing. No other president rose from lower depths of poverty, not even Lincoln.

Johnson was born December 29, 1808, in a two-room shack in Raleigh, **North Carolina**. Both of his parents were illiterate, and his father worked a variety of jobs to support the family. Service to the local militia as captain and to the Presbyterian Church made Johnson's father a respected member of his community. His death in December 1811 left Johnson's mother to struggle to support their two children on her own. She did so by sewing, weaving, and washing for a few years, and then she remarried. Her new husband proved to be a poor provider.

In 1822, Johnson and his brother were apprenticed to a local tailor. Johnson learned the trade well, and throughout his life remained proud of his skills. The tailor and local minister taught Johnson the basics of reading and writing. But the apprenticeship came to an abrupt end in 1824 when Johnson and his brother were involved in an incident of rowdiness. Fearing punishment, the boys fled to **Tennessee**, where Johnson eventually opened a tailor shop.

Soon after arriving in Greeneville, Tennessee, Johnson met Eliza McCardle. They were married May 17, 1827, and had five children. His tailor shop thrived, but Johnson's passion for political debate drew him into public service. In time, he became a full-time politician representing the working people. He was a tireless campaigner with excellent speaking skills, and he was both courageous and outspoken. His devotion to the common farmers and tradesmen of Tennessee and his work against the wealthy slaveholders moved him to support the U.S. **Constitution** and the union of states. Johnson, however, was also a man of the South who had firm proslavery beliefs.

Between 1829 and 1842, Johnson served as alderman and then mayor of Greeneville, and then as a state legislator. He next served as a member of the U.S. House of Representatives from 1843 to 1853. He was elected both in 1853 and 1855 to serve as the governor of Tennessee. In 1857, he won a seat in the U.S. Senate.

Ascending to the presidency

Johnson was a U.S. senator during the election of 1860, when the debates marked growing divisions in the nation. The expansion of **slavery** and state power to dictate federal government policy were two important issues. Johnson supported the proslavery candidate of the **Democratic Party**, Stephen A. Douglas (1813–1861), who lost the election to the Republican, Abraham Lincoln. Though Lincoln denounced the expansion of slavery, his party intended to allow it to remain in the areas where it had already been established.

Southern fears of losing the right to own slaves and to have powerful state governments led many states to consider **secession**, or leaving the union of the United States. Johnson's own state of Tennessee was one of them. As senator, Johnson spent the winter after the election trying to discourage secession, taking a much firmer pro-**Union** stand than most Southern congressmen. At first, Johnson was successful.

A month before Lincoln's inauguration in March 1861, six states seceded to form the **Confederate States of America**. In April, the Confederates fired upon the Union forces at Fort Sumter in **South Carolina**, provoking Lincoln to call for troops from the states. Tennessee joined the next wave of seceding states.

Johnson and his family were driven from Tennessee, but Johnson maintained his position within the U.S. Senate. Although he believed in states' rights and slavery, he placed preservation of the Union above all else. He denounced the Confederacy as a conspiracy by wealthy plantation owners, and he took an active role in devising war measures in the Senate. Johnson was the only Southern senator not to resign his seat and follow his state into the Confederacy.

In 1862, the Union army pushed Confederate forces out of western and central Tennessee. Noting Johnson's Union loyalty, Lincoln invited him to become the military governor of Tennessee. Johnson received full power to restore order in Tennessee and to build a new pro-Union government for the state. It was a challenging task, but Johnson was aggressive in making it happen.

Johnson became the ideal running mate for President Lincoln's reelection campaign in 1864. Though Johnson was a Democrat, he was firmly committed to the Union. Having him as the vice presidential candidate helped to attract support from both the northern prowar

Democrats and the border state Unionists. Lincoln and Johnson were elected and then inaugurated March 4, 1865.

The Civil War came to an end just days before President Lincoln was shot by an assassin on April 14, 1865. Johnson was sworn in as president only hours after Lincoln's death on April 15. Reintegration of the rebellious states had yet to be arranged, so the difficult tasks of restoring the Union fell to Johnson's administration. Both his aggressively stubborn actions and his Southern and Democratic roots caused tensions with the Republican Congress.

Johnson as president

Johnson's presidency was dominated by the issues surrounding Reconstruction. What would the rebellious states be required to do before being brought back into the Union? How would they prove their loyalty? What changes to their political systems would they have to make? Since slavery had been abolished, what would be the status of blacks legally, politically, and socially?

President Johnson introduced his Reconstruction program on May 29, 1865, with the unanimous approval of his cabinet. The program had two proclamations. The Amnesty Proclamation pardoned (forgave) all participants in the rebellion except for the highest-level leaders of the Confederacy and the very wealthy. Those not pardoned would have to apply to the president for restoration of their rights to vote and hold office. Those pardoned would have to take a loyalty oath. All property, except slaves, would be restored.

The second proclamation, which dealt specifically with North Carolina, set the pattern for the reintegration of all seceded states where pro-Union governments were not yet set up. Acting governors were to appoint temporary state officials and to recommend people for federal appointments. There would be conventions to write new state constitutions that had to support the abolition of slavery and nullify (cancel) the states' ordinances (declarations) of secession. Only those who had been eligible to vote in 1861 and had taken the new loyalty oath could vote. Unpardoned rebels and all blacks were barred from voting. Similar proclamations were made for **Mississippi**, South Carolina, **Florida**, **Georgia**, **Alabama**, and **Texas**.

During the summer of 1865, all of these states held constitutional conventions. South Carolina, however, refused to nullify its ordinance of secession, and Mississippi rejected the **Thirteenth Amendment** to the U.S. Constitution, which had abolished slavery. By the fall of 1865, the Southern states held state and congressional elections. Many of the winning candidates were actually ineligible to hold office under the Amnesty Proclamation. Johnson himself contributed to the ineffectiveness of this proclamation. At first, he granted pardons only sparingly, but by the end of 1865 he was granting them almost automatically in hopes of gaining goodwill in the South. He wanted to run for president in the election of 1868 and was already seeking political support.

When the mostly Republican U.S. Congress reconvened in 1866, they would not let the newly elected Southern congressmen take their seats. Congress created the Joint Committee of Fifteen on Reconstruction to investigate conditions in the South and to recommend appropriate laws. These actions were a signal to Johnson that Congress believed that further Reconstruction measures were needed. It was a direct challenge not only to Johnson's Reconstruction policy but also to his authority as president.

Johnson reacted to Congress by asking the public to pressure Congress to accept the Southern congressmen. For a time, it seemed that this strategy might work. In February 1866, however, Congress passed the Freedmen's Bureau Bill to extend indefinitely the **Freedmen's Bureau**, which had been established at the end of the Civil War to provide aid, education, and legal protection to former slaves. Before passing it, Republicans in Congress had offered to change anything that Johnson did not like about the bill, and since he had voiced no objections, they expected that he would sign it. However, when it came time for the president to sign the bill into law, Johnson stunned Congress by declaring it unnecessary and unconstitutional. The congressional vote on the bill had excluded the duly elected representatives of the eleven Southern states, and on that basis Johnson vetoed it. Congress failed to override the veto, and Johnson reveled publicly in the victory.

Three weeks later, Congress passed the **Civil Rights Act of 1866**, which declared that blacks were citizens of the United States entitled to equal protection of the laws. It gave the federal government broad enforcement powers. Johnson vetoed this bill as well, calling it an unconstitutional intrusion on states' rights that discriminated against whites in favor of blacks. Although his opinion may have been sincere, Johnson's veto was motivated also by his desire to retain Democratic and Southern support. Outrage in Congress led it to override Johnson's veto, making the bill a law. This was the first time in American history that Congress had overridden a presidential veto.

Impeachment

Johnson's vetoes and unwillingness to compromise united his political opponents in Congress. This weakened Johnson's power during the remainder of his term. In total, Johnson used the veto twenty-nine times, and Congress overrode it fifteen times. The veto overrides enacted many Reconstruction acts and the Tenure of Office Act. This act prohibited the president from dismissing, without Senate approval, any federal official previously appointed with the Senate's consent. Johnson called it an unconstitutional violation of the powers of the presidency.

Johnson had inherited his entire cabinet from Lincoln. From the start, he had been working with the cabinet members' guidance, but he did not work well with Secretary of War Edwin Stanton (1814–1869). Though Johnson had tolerated Stanton's lack of respect for his policies, by the summer of 1867, the president moved to suspend him. As Congress was out of session, Johnson replaced Stanton temporarily with former Civil War general **Ulysses S. Grant** (1822–1885). Upon reconvening, Congress rejected Johnson's appointment. In February 1868, Johnson again removed Stanton from office and replaced him with General Lorenzo Thomas (1804–1875). Ignoring the need for Senate approval, Johnson violated the Tenure of Office Act.

Johnson's disregard for the law gave a dissatisfied Congress the excuse it wanted to pursue impeachment. Impeachment is the first of a two-step process to remove a government official without his or her consent. The process begins with an accusation of misconduct from the House of Representatives (impeachment), and continues with a trial in the Senate (resulting in possible conviction). The proceedings took all of April and May 1868, and though the House voted to impeach Johnson, the president narrowly escaped conviction in the Senate. Seven Republican senators repeatedly cast "not-guilty" votes, consistently leaving the opposition one vote short of removing Johnson from the White House. Though Johnson remained in office, he stopped aggressively frustrating the efforts of the Republican Congress.

Post-presidential years

Johnson pursued the Democratic nomination for president in 1868. However, his battles with Congress, his poor presidential record, and the impeachment all worked against him. The Republicans had nominated a popular war hero, General Grant, and the Democrats needed a stronger candidate to face the opposition. They chose New York governor Horatio Seymour (1810–1886), but Grant won easily.

Johnson left the White House on the morning of Grant's inauguration, March 4, 1869. He returned to Greeneville, Tennessee, where he again threw himself into local and state Democratic affairs. He failed in his efforts to be elected to the U.S. Senate in 1869 and to the U.S. House of Representatives in 1872. In 1875, the Tennessee legislature finally elected Johnson to the U.S. Senate by one vote. Johnson entered office in March 1875, but his service proved to be short. On July 28, he suffered a stroke, then he suffered another a few days later and died on July 31, 1875.

Lyndon B. Johnson

Lyndon B. Johnson was born on August 27, 1908, into a political family on a **Texas** farm. Never a serious student, Johnson focused more on being popular. After high school graduation, he held a number of part-time jobs and hitchhiked to **California** with friends. Once there, he discovered that his dream of a high-paying job was just a dream, and he hitchhiked back to Texas. At that point, Johnson decided college was the best way to go, and he enrolled in Southwest Texas State Teachers College. He graduated in three years and got a teaching job in Houston.

Politics was in his blood, however, and by November 1931 Johnson was working for a congressional candidate named Richard Kleberg (1887–1955). Kleberg won the race and took Johnson with him to **Washington, D.C.**, as his personal secretary. Twenty-three-year-old Johnson spent the next four years building a network of friends and contacts in Washington. He met and married Claudia Alta Taylor in 1934. The couple eventually had two daughters.

The following year, U.S. president **Franklin D. Roosevelt** (1882–1945; served 1933–45) chose Johnson to head the Texas division of the National Youth Administration (NYA), a program that provided education and employment assistance to young people. He was the

837

After President John F. Kennedy's assassination, Lyndon B. Johnson (above) became president. His presidency was riddled with conflict as a result of U.S. participation in the Vietnam War. AP IMAGES

youngest of the state NYA chiefs, and he won widespread praise for his work.

Heads to the Senate

Johnson won election to the U.S. House of Representatives in 1937, beating eight other candidates. He remained in the House for more than ten years. In 1948, he ran for U.S. Senate and won.

Johnson was elected Senate leader of the Democratic minority in 1953. When the Democrats won control of the Senate from the Republicans in 1954, he became the Senate majority leader, an influential position he retained for six years.

Johnson ran for the Democratic nomination in the presidential race of 1960 but lost to U.S. senator **John F. Kennedy** (1917–1963). Kennedy asked Johnson to be his vice presidential running mate and Johnson accepted. In November, Kennedy was elected president after defeating incumbent vice president **Richard Nixon** (1913–1994). When Kennedy was assassinated on November 22, 1963, Johnson took the oath of office and became the thirty-sixth president of the United States.

President Johnson

Kennedy had been an extremely popular president, and the nation mourned his death. Johnson needed to assure the public that he could fill his predecessor's shoes, but at the same time, he was dealing with an administration of intellectuals from the Northeast who viewed Johnson as an unrefined southerner who did not have what it takes to lead the country.

Johnson delivered a televised speech to Congress just days after Kennedy's funeral, and with it he won both sympathy and support. He became popular enough to win reelection in 1964. That popularity also convinced Congress to pass numerous laws to help America's minorities and poor. Together, these laws made up a program known as the "**Great Society**."

Trouble brews

Despite the president's efforts in civil rights and the "war on poverty," there were summer riots in cities across America from 1964 to 1968. (See **Race Riots of the 1960s**.) In the background was another disaster waiting to happen: the **Vietnam War** (1959–75).

Vietnam was a problem Johnson inherited from Kennedy and the thirty-fourth president, **Dwight D. Eisenhower** (1890–1969; served 1953–61). Since the 1950s, America had backed the South Vietnamese government in its war against the North Vietnamese communist government. With the support of China and the Soviet Union, North Vietnam hoped to take control of South Vietnam.

Just before Kennedy's assassination in 1963, the leader of South Vietnam was assassinated. The government there became weaker and more unstable. North Vietnam became more powerful and even won support among the South Vietnamese people.

America at war

In his 1964 campaign, Johnson had promised to keep American soldiers off the battlefields in Vietnam. Privately, however, he had every intention of sending troops to fight. Like other leaders before him, Johnson believed in the **domino theory**, which says if one country falls to communism, those surrounding it will, too. Johnson did not want to take the blame for communist victory in Vietnam.

In August 1964, North Vietnamese forces reportedly attacked two American destroyer ships in the Tonkin Gulf off the coast of North Vietnam. Congress gave Johnson power to do whatever he felt necessary to prevent further aggression. Years later, it became known that the United States had provoked the attack by invading North Vietnamese waters to aid South Vietnamese. In addition to keeping this secrect, Johnson also exaggerated the attack on the destroyers. In fact, he had already prepared what became known as the Tonkin Gulf Resolution and was just waiting for the right time to use it.

Johnson sent troops to Vietnam with an official declaration of war. With each passing year, he sent over more American troops, spurring a major **antiwar movement** in the United States. By 1966, Congress was also against the war. By promising the public that victory was just around the corner when in reality the war was far from over, Johnson created what was known as the "credibility gap." The war he publicly described was far different—and more optimistic—than the one portrayed in the media. Public trust of the president was destroyed.

Leaves the White House

Even Johnson had to admit his ineffectiveness as a leader. On March 31, 1968 (an election year), Johnson stunned the nation by announcing that he would not seek nomination of the **Democratic Party** for another presidential term. This voluntary stepping-down earned Johnson the admiration of the public and media, as did his announcement that he was calling a temporary halt in the bombing of North Vietnam. Although the war continued, bombing in North Vietnam never did resume.

Johnson retired to his Texas ranch, where he wrote his memoirs. A heart attack in 1955 left him in fragile health, and afterwards he experienced regular heart trouble. In January 1973, Johnson suffered another heart attack and died at home.

Mother Jones

Mary Harris Jones was born in Ireland in either 1830 or 1837 (records vary) and came to the United States as a young woman. She met and married George Jones, who, along with their four children, died of yellow fever in 1867. Jones moved to Chicago, **Illinois**, and lost everything she owned four years later in the Great Chicago Fire.

Jones needed to support herself so she joined the **Knights of Labor**, a labor union, and worked on its behalf to gain acceptance in the public and grow its numbers. Her time was spent rallying support and speaking out on behalf of the working class. In 1905, she helped found a labor union called Industrial Workers of the World (IWW), also known as the Wobblies. Jones became an organizer of labor strikes throughout America but had a particular fondness for miners and their cause. Of all the workers, miners experienced by far the worst (and most dangerous) working conditions and the lowest wages; Jones made it her personal mission to help them achieve better lives.

Jones worked not only with miners but also with their wives and children. She would organize mining families to participate in demonstrations and protests on behalf of the miners. Women and children carrying mops and brooms marched at the mines, preventing strikebreakers from crossing the miners' picket lines into the mine shafts. Jones earned the nickname "Mother" when she began calling the miners her "boys."

Mother Jones embraced socialism (an economic system in which the government owns and operates business and production as well as controls the distribution of wealth) and worked closely with American Railway Union leader Eugene Debs (1855–1926). An enthusiastic public speaker, she was known for organizing public events to get the media focused on striking workers. Her tireless efforts on behalf of working men and women took her to the coal mines of **Pennsylvania**, where she encouraged miners to join the union.

Activist Mother Jones was known for organizing public events to get the media focused on striking workers. THE LIBRARY OF CONGRESS

Opponents of Jones called her the most dangerous woman in America; her physical courage was known throughout the nation. She joined in protests, many of which resulted in her arrest. Jones spent time in more jails throughout the country than any other labor activist in history.

Surprisingly, Jones did not support the **women's suffrage movement** (the right to vote). She believed that a focus on winning the vote would take away much-needed attention on the economic situation of working-class women. Jones discussed this in her autobiography, *The Autobiography of Mother Jones*. In it, she wrote, "You don't need a vote to raise hell, you need convictions and a voice."

Mother Jones died in 1930 at the age of ninety-three or one hundred. She is buried in the Union Miners Cemetery in Mount Olive, Illinois. Thousands of miners and their families attended her funeral. Her name lives on as the title of a political magazine that supports socialism. Jones is remembered as the "Grandmother of All Agitators."

Lower Courts

The Constitution says that Congress may create courts inferior to the Supreme Court. Congress has divided the United States into twelve circuits, eleven of them numbered and one covering the District of Columbia. These circuits each have one circuit court of appeals and many district courts. The district courts, which hold trials, are scattered throughout the states in federal districts. The circuit courts of appeals hear appeals from the district courts. Parties who lose in the circuit courts of appeals may ask the Supreme Court to review the case.

Judicial Branch

The U.S. **Constitution** divides the federal government into three branches. The judicial branch, headed by the **Supreme Court**, decides cases under the nation's laws. The other two branches are the **legislative branch**, called Congress, and the **executive branch**, headed by the president of the United States.

Most of the Constitution's provisions concerning the judicial branch appear in Article III, which begins, "The judicial power of the United States, shall be vested in one Supreme Court, and in such inferior courts as the Congress may from time to time ordain and establish." The Constitution does not list any qualifications that a person must meet in order to be a judge.

Judicial power is the power to decide cases that arise under the U.S. Constitution, federal laws, and treaties with foreign nations. It also covers other kinds of cases, such as those affecting ambassadors, public ministers, and consuls; cases involving the seas; cases in which the United States is a party; and cases between different states or between citizens of different states.

The Constitution distinguishes between original jurisdiction and appellate jurisdiction. Original jurisdiction is the power to hold a trial to make a first decision in a case. The Supreme Court's original jurisdiction power only covers cases in which a state is a party, and cases affecting ambassadors, public ministers, and consuls. In all other cases, the Supreme Court has only appellate jurisdiction, which is the power to review decisions from lower courts for errors.

The Constitution says that trials for all crimes must be heard by juries, and must be held in the same state in which the crime was committed. No person may be convicted of the crime of treason except by confession in court, or by evidence that includes testimony from at least two persons concerning the specific act of treason.

Where to Learn More

In addition to numerous U•X•L publications, the following sources were used to help compile the entries in this book.

Books

Altman, Linda Jacobs. *The American Civil Rights Movement: The African American Struggle for Equality.* Berkeley Heights, NJ: Enslow, 2004.

Ambrose, Stephen E. *Undaunted Courage: The Pioneering First Mission to Explore America's Wild Frontier.* New York: Pocket Books, 2003.

Anbinder, Tyler. *Nativism and Slavery: The Northern Know Nothings and the Politics of the 1850s.* New York: Oxford University Press, 1992.

Anderson, Terry H. *The Movement and the Sixties.* New York: Oxford University Press, 1996.

Anderson, Terry H. *The Pursuit of Fairness: A History of Affirmative Action.* New York: Oxford University Press, 2004.

Arsenault, Raymond. *Freedom Riders: 1961 and the Struggle for Racial Justice.* New York: Oxford University Press, 2006.

Bailey, Anne C. *African Voices of the Atlantic Slave Trade: Beyond the Silence and the Shame.* Boston: Beacon Press, 2006.

Baker, H. Robert. *The Rescue of Joshua Glover: A Fugitive Slave, the Constitution, and the Coming of the Civil War.* Athens: Ohio University Press, 2007.

Baker, Jean H. *James Buchanan.* New York: Times Books, 2004.

Barilleaux, Ryan J., and Mark J. Rozell. *Power and Prudence: The Presidency of George H. W. Bush.* College Station: Texas A&M University, 2004.

Barnes, Catherine A. *Journey from Jim Crow: the Desegregation of Southern Transit.* New York: Columbia University Press, 1983.

Bass, Patrik Henry. *Like a Mighty Stream: The March on Washington, August 28, 1963.* Philadelphia: Running Press, 2003.

Bates, Daisy. *The Long Shadow of Little Rock: A Memoir,* reprint ed. Fayetteville: University of Arkansas Press, 1987 (orig. pub. 1962).

Bauer, K. Jack. *Zachary Taylor: Soldier, Planter, Statesman of the Old Southwest.* Baton Rouge: Louisiana State University Press, 1985.

Beals, Melba Pattillo. *Warriors Don't Cry: Searing Memoir of Battle to Integrate Little Rock,* reprint ed. New York: Washington Square Press, 1995.

Beckwith, Francis J., and Todd E. Jones, eds. *Affirmative Action: Social Justice or Reverse Discrimination.* Amherst, NH: Prometheus Books, 1997.

Benn, Carl. *The War of 1812.* London: Routledge, 2003.

Berlin, Ira. *Many Thousands Gone: The First Two Centuries of Slavery in North America.* Cambridge, MA: Harvard University Press, 1998.

Bernstein, Peter L. *Wedding of the Waters: The Erie Canal and the Making of a Great Nation.* New York: W. W. Norton, 2005.

Bernstein, R. B. *Thomas Jefferson.* New York: Oxford University Press, 2003.

Bernstein, Richard. *Out of the Blue: A Narrative of September 11, 2001.* New York: Times Books, 2002.

Binder, Frederick Moore. *James Buchanan and the American Empire.* Selinsgrove, PA: Susquehanna University Press, 1994.

Blassingame, John W. *The Slave Community: Plantation Life in the Antebellum South.* New York: Oxford University Press, 1979.

Blue, Frederick J. *No Taint of Compromise: Crusaders in Antislavery Politics.* Baton Rouge: Louisiana State University Press, 2006.

Bonilla, Denise M. *School Violence.* New York: H. W. Wilson, 2000.

Bordewich, Fergus M. *Bound for Canaan, the Epic Story of the Underground Railroad: America's First Civil Rights Movement.* New York: Amistad, 2006.

Borneman, Walter R. *1812: The War That Forged a Nation.* New York: HarperCollins, 2004.

Bowen, Catherine Drinker. *Miracle at Philadelphia: The Story of the Constitutional Convention—May to September, 1787.* Boston: Little, Brown, 1966.

Bowen, William G., and Derek Bok. *The Shape of the River: Long Term Consequences of Considering Race in College and University Admissions.* Princeton, NJ: Princeton University Press, 1998.

Branch, Taylor. *At Canaan's Edge: America in the King Years, 1965–68.* New York: Simon & Schuster, 2006.

Branch, Taylor. *Pillar of Fire: America in the King Years, 1963–65.* New York: Simon & Schuster, 1998.

Brands, H. W. *The Age of Gold: The California Gold Rush and the New American Dream.* New York: Anchor, 2003.

Brands, H. W. *Andrew Jackson: His Life and Times.* New York: Anchor Books, 2006.

Brill, Marlene Targ. *James Buchanan: Fifteenth President of the United States.* Chicago: Childrens Press, 1988.

Buechler, Steven M. *Women's Movements in the United States: Woman Suffrage, Equal Rights, and Beyond.* New Brunswick, NJ: Rutgers University Press, 2007.

Burgan, Michael. *The Missouri Compromise.* Mankato, MN: Compass Point Books, 2006.

Burns, Stewart, ed. *Daybreak of Freedom: The Montgomery Bus Boycott.* Chapel Hill: University of North Carolina Press, 1997.

Bush, George. *All the Best, George Bush: My Life in Letters and Other Writings.* New York: Scribner, 1999.

Bush, George, and Brent Scowcroft. *A World Transformed.* New York: Knopf, 1998.

Cable, Mary. *Black Odyssey: The Case of the Slave Ship Amistad.* New York: Penguin Books, 1977.

Cagin, Seth, and Philip Dray. *We Are Not Afraid: The Story of Goodman, Schwerner, and Chaney and the Civil Rights Campaign for Mississippi.* New York: Bantam, 1991.

Carlisle, Rodney P., and John Stewart Bowman. *Perisan Gulf War.* New York: Facts on File, 2003.

Carnoy, Martin, et al. *The New Global Economy in the Information Age: Reflections on Our Changing World.* University Park: Pennsylvania State University Press, 1993.

Carson, Clayborn. *In Struggle: SNCC and the Black Awakening of the 1960s.* Cambridge, MA: Harvard University Press, 1995.

Carson, Clayborn, and Martin Luther King Jr. *Autobiography of Martin Luther King, Jr.* New York: Warner Books, 1998.

Chafe, William Henry, Raymond Gavins, and Robert Korstad, eds. *Remembering Jim Crow: African Americans Tell About Life in the Segregated South.* New York: New Press, 2003.

Clinton, Bill. *My Life.* New York: Knopf, 2004.

Colaiaco, James A. *Frederick Douglass and the Fourth of July.* New York: Palgrave Macmillan, 2007.

Colbert, Nancy A. *Great Society: The Story of Lyndon Baines Johnson.* Greensboro, NC: Morgan Reynolds, 2002.

Crapol, Edward P. *John Tyler, the Accidental President.* Chapel Hill: University of North Carolina Press, 2006.

Cunningham, Noble. *In Pursuit of Reason: The Life of Thomas Jefferson.* Baton Rouge: Louisiana State University Press, 1987.

Dallek, Robert. *Flawed Giant: Lyndon B. Johnson, 1960–1973.* Oxford: Oxford University Press, 1998.

Daniels, Roger. *Coming to America: A History of Immigration and Ethnicity in American Life.* New York: HarperCollins, 1990.

Darmer, M. Katherine B., Robert M. Baird, and Stuart E. Rosenbaum, eds. *Civil Liberties vs. National Security: In a Post 9/11 World.* Amherst, NY: Prometheus Books, 2004.

Davis, William C. *Lone Star Rising: The Revolutionary Birth of the Texas Republic.* College Station: Texas A&M University Press, 2006.

DiConsiglio, John. *Franklin Pierce: America's Fourteenth President.* Chicago: Childrens Press, 2004.

Dimond, Paul R. *Beyond Busing: Reflections on Urban Segregation, the Courts, and Equal Opportunity.* Ann Arbor: University of Michigan Press, 2005.

Douglas, Davison M. *Reading, Writing and Race: The Desegregation of the Charlotte Schools.* Chapel Hill: University of North Carolina, 1995.

Douglass, Frederick. *Narrative of the Life of Frederick Douglass.* Clayton, DE: Prestwick House, 2004.

Dyson, Michael Eric. *Making Malcolm: The Myth and Meaning of Malcolm X.* New York, Oxford University Press, 1995.

Egerton, Douglas R. *He Shall Go Out Free: The Lives of Denmark Vesey,* rev. ed. Lanham, MD: Rowman & Littlefield Publishers, 2004.

Ellis, Joseph J. *American Sphinx: The Character of Thomas Jefferson.* New York: Vintage, 1998.

Eskew, Glenn T. *But for Birmingham: The Local and National Movements in the Civil Rights Struggle.* Chapel Hill: University of North Carolina Press, 1997.

Etzioni, Amitai. *How Patriotic Is the Patriot Act? Freedom vs. Security in the Age of Terrorism.* Oxford, UK: Routledge, 2004.

Fairclough, Adam. *To Redeem the Soul of America: The Southern Christian Leadership Conference and Martin Luther King, Jr.* Athens: University of Georgia Press, 2001.

Farber, David R., and Beth L. Bailey. *The Columbia Guide to America in the 1960s.* New York: Columbia University Press, 2003.

Farmer, James. *Lay Bare the Heart: An Autobiography of the Civil Rights Movement.* New York: Penguin/Plume, 1986.

Fenton, William N. *The Great Law and the Longhouse: A Political History of the Iroquois Confederacy.* Tulsa: University of Oklahoma Press, 1998.

Finlayson, Reggie. *We Shall Overcome: The History of the American Civil Rights Movement.* Minneapolis, MN: Lerner, 2002.

Fitzgerald, Stephanie. *Little Rock Nine: Struggle for Integration.* Mankato, MN: Compass Point Books, 2006.

Flanagan, Alice K. *The Lowell Mill Girls.* Mankato, MN: Compass Point Books, 2005.

Fleming, Thomas. *The Louisiana Purchase.* Hoboken, NJ: Wiley, 2003.

Forbes, Robert Pierce. *The Missouri Compromise and Its Aftermath: Slavery and the Meaning of America.* Chapel Hill: University of North Carolina Press, 2007.

Franklin, John Hope, and Loren Schweninger. *Runaway Slaves: Rebels on the Plantation.* New York: Oxford University Press, 1999.

Frazier, Donald S., ed. *The United States and Mexico at War: Nineteenth-Century Expansionism and Conflict.* New York: Macmillan, 1998.

Freehling, William W. *Prelude to the Civil War: The Nullfication Controversy.* New York: HarperCollins, 1968.

Gara, Larry. *The Presidency of Franklin Pierce.* Lawrence: University Press of Kansas, 1991.

Garrow, David G. *Bearing the Cross: Martin Luther King and the Southern Leadership Conference.* Norwalk, CT: Easton Press, 1986.

Gitlin, Todd. *Years of Hope, Days of Rage,* rev. ed. New York: Bantam, 1993.

Goldman, Roger, and David Gallen, eds. *Thurgood Marshall: Justice for All.* New York: Carroll & Graf, 1992.

Gonzalez, Juan. *Harvest of Empire: A History of Latinos in America.* New York: Viking, 2000.

Good, Timothy S. *Lincoln-Douglas Debates and the Making of a President.* Jefferson, NC: McFarland, 2007.

Greenblatt, Miriam. *John Quincy Adams: Sixth President of the United States.* Ada, OK: Garrett Educational Corp., 1990

Greenburg, Cheryl Lynn. *A Circle of Trust: Remembering the SNCC.* Rutgers University Press, 2005.

Grofman, Bernard, ed. *Legacies of the 1964 Civil Rights Act.* Charlottesville: University of Virginia, 2000.

Gumbel, Andrew. *Steal This Vote: Dirty Elections and the Rotten History of Democracy in America.* New York: Nation Books, 2005.

Gurko, Miriam. *The Ladies of Seneca Falls: The Birth of the Women's Rights Movement.* New York: Pantheon, 1987.

Hacker, Andrew. *Two Nations: Black and White, Separate, Hostile, Unequal.* New York: Ballantine Books, 1995.

Haley, Alex. *The Autobiography of Malcolm X.* New York, Grove Press, 1965.

Harms, Robert W. *The Diligent: A Voyage Through the Worlds of the Slave Trade.* New York: Basic Books, 2001.

Hasday, Judy L. *The Civil Rights Act of 1964: An End to Racial Segregation.* New York: Chelsea House, 2007.

Haugen, Brenda. *Frederick Douglass: Slave, Writer, Abolitionist.* Mankato, MN: Compass Point Books, 2005.

Haynes, Sam W. *James K. Polk and the Expansionist Impulse.* Edited by Oscar Handlin. New York: Longman, 1997.

Haynes, Sam W., and Christopher Morris, eds. *Manifest Destiny and Empire: American Antebellum Expansionism.* College Station: Texas A&M University Press, 1997.

Hendrick, George. *Why Not Every Man?: African Americans and Civil Disobedience in the Quest for the Dream.* Chicago: Ivan R. Dee, 2005.

Hickey, Donald R. *The War of 1812: A Forgotten Conflict.* Urbana: University of Illinois Press, 1989.

Higginson, Thomas Wentworth. *Black Rebellion: Five Slave Revolts.* Cambridge, MA: Da Capo Press, 2001.

Hindle, Brooke, and Steven Lubar. *Engines of Change: The American Industrial Revolution, 1790–1860.* Albany: State University of New York Press, 1981.

Hinks, Peter. *Encyclopedia of Antislavery and Abolition.* Westport, CT: Greenwood Press, 2006.

Howard-Pitney, David. *Martin Luther King, Jr., Malcolm X, and the Civil Rights Struggle of the 1950s and 1960s: A Brief History with Documents.* New York: Bedford/St. Martin's, 2004.

Hulnick, Arthur S. *Keeping Us Safe: Secret Intelligence and Homeland Security.* Westport, CT: Praeger, 2004.

Hunter, Tera W. *To 'Joy My Freedom: Southern Black Women's Lives and Labors After the Civil War,* reprint ed. Cambridge, MA: Harvard University Press, 1998.

Isenberg, Irwin, ed. *The City in Crisis.* New York: H. W. Wilson, 1968.

Jaffa, Harry V. *Crisis of the House Divided: An Interpretation of the Issues in the Lincoln-Douglas Debates.* Chicago: University of Chicago Press, 1982.

Johnson, Susan Lee. *Roaring Camp: The Social World of the California Gold Rush.* New York: W. W. Norton, 2001.

Jones, Howard. *Mutiny on the Amistad: The Saga of a Slave Revolt and Its Impact on American Abolition, Law, and Diplomacy.* New York: Oxford University Press, 1987.

Joseph, Peniel E. *Waiting 'Til the Midnight Hour: A Narrative History of Black Power in America.* Austin, TX: Holt, 2007.

Josephy, Alvin M., Jr. *Lewis and Clark Through Indian Eyes.* New York: Knopf, 2006.

Jurmain, Suzanne. *Freedom's Sons: The True Story of the Amistad Mutiny.* New York: HarperCollins, 1998.

Kagan, Elena, and Cass R. Sunstein. *Remembering "TM."* Chicago: University of Chicago Press, 1993.

Kaplan, Leonard V., and Beverly I. Moran, eds. *Aftermath: The Clinton Impeachment and the Presidency in the Age of Political Spectacle.* New York: New York University Press, 2001.

Kearns, Doris. *Lyndon Johnson and the American Dream.* New York: St. Martin's Griffin, 1991.

Kent, Zachary. *The Persian Gulf War: The "Mother of All Battles."* Berkeley Heights, NJ: Enslow, 2000.

King, Martin Luther, Jr. *Letter from the Birmingham Jail.* San Francisco: Harper, 1994.

Klausmeyer, David. *Oregon Trail Stories: True Accounts of Life in a Covered Wagon.* Emeryville, CA: Falcon, 2003.

Klees, Emerson. *The Iroquois Confederacy: Legends and History.* New York: Cameo Press, 2003.

Kornblith, Gary G. *The Industrial Revolution in America.* Boston: Houghton Mifflin, 1998.

Kukla, Jon. *A Wilderness So Immense: The Louisiana Purchase and the Destiny of America.* New York: Anchor, 2004.

Kupperman, Karen Ordahl. *Roanoke: The Abandoned Colony,* 2nd ed. Lanham, MD: Rowman & Littlefield, 2007.

Langford, R. Everett. *Introduction to Weapons of Mass Destruction: Radiological, Chemical, and Biological.* Hoboken, NJ: Wiley-Interscience, 2004.

Lavender, David Sievert. *Snowbound: The Tragic Story of the Donner Party.* New York: Holiday House, 1996.

Levin, John, and Jack Levin. *Domestic Terrorism.* New York: Chelsea House, 2006.

Levinson, Sanford, and Bartholomew Sparrow, eds. *The Louisiana Purchase and American Expansion, 1803–1898.* Lanham, MD: Rowman & Littlefield, 2005.

Levitas, Daniel. *The Terrorist Next Door: The Militia Movement and the Radical Right.* New York: St. Martin's Griffin, 2004.

Lewis, Meriwether, and William Clark. *The Journals of Lewis and Clark.* Edited by Bernard De Voto. Boston: Houghton Mifflin, 1953.

Lillegard, Dee. *James K. Polk: Eleventh President of the United States.* New York: Children's Press, 1988.

Linenthal, Edward T. *An Unfinished Bombing: Oklahoma City in American Memory.* New York: Oxford University Press, 2001.

Loevy, Robert D. *The Civil Rights Act of 1964: The Passage of the Law That Ended Racial Segregation.* Albany: State University of New York Press, 1997.

Lukas, J. Anthony. *Common Ground: A Turbulent Decade in the Lives of Three American Families.* New York: Vintage, 1986.

Madison, James. *Notes of Debates in the Federal Convention of 1787 Reported by James Madison.* New York: W. W. Norton, 1987.

Maxwell, Bruce. *Homeland Security: A Documentary History.* Washington, DC: CQ Press, 2004.

Mayer, Henry. *All on Fire: William Lloyd Garrison and the Abolition of Slavery.* New York: St. Martin's Griffin, 2000.

McAdam, Doug. *Freedom Summer.* New York: Oxford University Press, 1988.

McClymer, John F. *Mississippi Freedom Summer.* Detroit: Wadsworth, 2003.

McLynn, Frank. *Wagons West: The Epic Story of America's Overland Trails.* New York: Grove Press, 2002.

McPherson, Stephanie Sammartino. *"Lau v. Nichols": Bilingual Education in Public Schools.* Berkeley Heights, NJ: Enslow, 2000.

McWhorter, Diane. *Carry Me Home: Birmingham, Alabama: The Climactic Battle of the Civil Rights Revolution.* New York: Simon and Schuster, 2002.

Meed, Douglas V. *The Mexican War 1846–1848.* London, UK: Routledge, 2003.

Michael, George. *Confronting Right Wing Extremism and Terrorism in the USA.* New York: Routledge, 2003.

Miller, Douglas T. *Thomas Jefferson and the Creation of America.* New York: Facts on File, 1997.

Montejano, David. *Anglos and Mexicans in the Making of Texas, 1836–1986.* Austin: University of Texas Press, 1986.

Morganstein, Martin, Joan H. Cregg, and the Erie Canal Museum. *Erie Canal.* Mount Pleasant, SC: Arcadia, 2001.

Morris, Dick, and Eileen McGann. *Because He Could.* New York: HarperCollins, 2004.

Morrison, Toni. *Remember: The Journey to School Integration.* Boston: Houghton Mifflin, 2004.

Murphy, Jim. *Inside the Alamo.* New York: Delacorte Books, 2003.

Murphy, Virginia Reed. *Across the Plains in the Donner Party.* North Haven, CT: Linnet Books, 1996.

Myers, Walter Dean. *Amistad: A Long Road to Freedom,* reprint ed. New York: Puffin, 2001.

Myers, Walter Dean. *Malcolm X: By Any Means Necessary,* reprint ed. Bainbridge Island, WA: Polaris, 1999.

Nagel, Paul C. *John Quincy Adams: A Public Life, a Private Life.* New York: Knopf, 1997.

Newell, Clayton R. *The A to Z of the Persian Gulf War, 1990–91.* Lanham, MD: Scarecrow, 2007.

Nichols, Roy F. *Franklin Pierce: Young Hickory of the Granite Hills,* 2nd ed. Easton Press, 1988.

Niven, John. *John C. Calhoun and the Price of Union.* Baton Rouge: Louisiana State University Press, 1993.

Northrup, David, ed. *The Atlantic Slave Trade,* rev. ed. Boston: Houghton Mifflin, 2005.

Okin, J. R. *The Information Revolution: The Not-for-dummies Guide to the History, Technology, and Use of the World Wide Web.* Winter Harbor, ME: Ironbound Press, 2005.

Otfinoski, Steven. *William Henry Harrison: America's Ninth President.* Chicago: Children's Press, 2003.

Owsley, Frank Lawrence, Jr. *Struggle for the Gulf Borderlands: The Creek War and the Battle of New Orleans, 1812–1815.* Gainesville: University of Florida Press, 1981.

Packard, Jerrold M. *American Nightmare: The History of Jim Crow.* New York: St. Martin's Griffin, 2003.

Painter, Nell Irvin. *Sojourner Truth: A Life, A Symbol.* New York: W. W. Norton, 1997.

Pastan, Amy. *Martin Luther King, Jr.* New York: Dorling Kindersley, 2005.

Pauley, Garth E. *LBJ's American Promise: The 1965 Voting Rights Address.* College Station: Texas A&M University Press, 2007.

Peterson, Norma Lois. *The Presidencies of William Henry Harrison and John Tyler.* Lawrence: University Press of Kansas, 1989.

Postma, Johannes. *The Atlantic Slave Trade.* Gainesville: University Press of Florida, 2005.

Price, Richard. *Maroon Societies: Rebel Slave Communities in the Americas.* Baltimore, MD: Johns Hopkins University Press, 1996.

Ransom, Roger L. *Conflict and Compromise: The Political Economy of Slavery, Emancipation, and the American Civil War.* New York: Cambridge University Press, 2002.

Remini, Robert V. *John Quincy Adams.* New York: Times Books, 2002.

Riches, William T. Martin. *The Civil Rights Movement: Struggle and Resistance.* New York: St. Martin's, 1997.

Richter, Daniel K. *The Ordeal of the Longhouse: The Peoples of the Iroquois League in the Era of European Colonization.* Chapel Hill: University of North Carolina Press, 1992.

Ricks, Thomas E. *Fiasco: The American Military Adventure in Iraq.* New York: Penguin, 2007.

Rife, Douglas. *History Speaks: Seneca Falls Declaration of Sentiments and Resolutions.* Carthage, IL: Teaching and Learning Co., 2002.

Roberts, Jeremy. *Zachary Taylor.* Minneapolis, MN: Lerner Publications, 2005.

Romano, Renee Christine, and Leigh Raiford. *The Civil Rights Movement in American Memory.* Athens: University of Georgia Press, 2006.

Ross, Jim, and Paul Myers. *We Will Never Forget: Eyewitness Accounts of the Oklahoma City Federal Building Bombing.* Waco, TX: Eakin Press, 1996.

Russo, Peggy A., and Paul Finkelman. *Terrible Swift Sword: The Legacy of John Brown.* Athens: Ohio University Press, 2005.

Rutland, Robert A. *James Madison: The Founding Father.* New York: Macmillan, 1987.

San Miguel, Gaudalupe, Jr. *Contested Policy: The Rise and Fall of Federal Bilingual Education in the United States, 1960–2001.* University of North Texas Press, 2004.

Schwartz, Marie Jenkins. *Born in Bondage: Growing Up Enslaved in the Antebellum South.* Cambridge, MA: Harvard University Press, 2001.

Scott, Darrell, Beth Nimmo, and Steve Rabey. *Rachel's Tears: The Spiritual Journey of Columbine Martyr Rachel Scott.* Nashville, TN: Thomas Nelson, 2000.

Scott, John A., and Robert Alan Scott. *John Brown of Harpers Ferry.* New York: Facts on File, 1993.

Shapiro, Andrew L. *The Control Revolution: How the Internet Is Putting Individuals in Charge and Changing the World We Know.* New York: PublicAffairs, 2000.

Shaw, Ronald E. *Canals for a Nation: The Canal Era in the United States, 1790–1860.* Lexington: University Press of Kentucky, 1990.

Siebert, Wibur H. *The Underground Railroad from Slavery to Freedom: A Comprehensive History.* Mineola, NY: Dover Publications, 2006.

Siegenthaler, John. *James Polk: 1845–49.* New York: Times Books, 2003.

Sitkoff, Harvard. *The Struggle for Black Equality, 1954–1992.* New York: Hill and Wang, 1993.

Smith, Dennis. *Report from Ground Zero: The Story of the Rescue Efforts at the World Trade Center.* New York: Viking, 2002.

Smith, Elbert B. *The Presidencies of Zachary Taylor and Millard Fillmore.* Lawrence: University Press of Kansas, 1988.

Smith, Mark M. *Debating Slavery: Economy and Society in the Antebellum American South.* New York: Cambridge University Press, 2004.

Stefoff, Rebecca. *Andrew Jackson: Seventh President of the United States.* Ada, OK: Garrett Educational Corp., 1988.

Stegner, Page. *Winning the Wild West: The Epic Saga of the American Frontier, 1800–1899.* New York: Free Press, 2002.

Stevens, Carol B., ed. *William Henry Harrison.* Westport, CT: Greenwood Publishing Group, 1998.

Stewart, George R. *Ordeal by Hunger: The Story of the Donner Party,* rev. ed. New York: Adventure Library, 2002 (orig. pub. 1936).

Stick, David. *Roanoke Island: The Beginnings of English America.* Chapel Hill: University of North Carolina Press, 1983.

Stone, Geoffrey R. *Perilous Times: Free Speech in Wartime from the Sedition Act of 1798 to the War on Terrorism.* New York: W. W. Norton, 2004.

Street, Paul. *Segregated Schools: Educational Apartheid in Post–Civil Rights America.* London, UK: Routledge, 2005.

Stuart, Reginald C. *United States Expansionism and British North America, 1775–1871.* Chapel Hill: University of North Carolina Press, 1988.

Taylor, Eric Robert. *If We Must Die: Shipboard Insurrections in the Era of the Atlantic Slave Trade.* Baton Rouge: Louisiana State University Press, 2006.

Telgen, Diane. *Brown v. Board of Education.* Detroit: Omnigraphics, 2005.

Thompson, Frank T. *The Alamo.* Denton: University of North Texas Press, 2005.

Thompson, William, and Dorcas Thompson. *The Spanish Exploration of Florida: The Adventures of the Spanish Conquistadors.* Broomall, PA: Mason Crest, 2002.

Thoreau, Henry David. *Walden and "Civil Disobedience."* New York: Signet, 1960.

Time writers. *The Monsters Next Door: A Special Report on the Colorado School Massacre.* New York: Time Inc., 1999.

Truth, Sojourner. *Narrative of Sojourner Truth: A Bondswoman of Olden Time, with a History of Her Labors and Correspondence Drawn from Her "Book of Life."* New York: Oxford University Press, 1994.

Tushnet, Mark V. *Making Civil Rights Law: Thurgood Marshall and the Supreme Court, 1936–1961.* New York: Oxford University Press, 1994.

Tushnet, Mark V., ed. *Thurgood Marshall: His Speeches, Writings, Arguments, Opinions and Reminiscences.* Chicago: Lawrence Hill Books, 2001.

Vallelly, Richard M. *The Voting Rights Act: Securing the Ballot.* Washington, DC: CQ Press, 2005.

Walker, Dale L. *Eldorado: The California Gold Rush.* New York: Forge Books, 2003.

Walker, Jane C. *John Tyler: A President of Many Firsts.* Granville, OH: McDonald and Woodward, 2001.

Weatherman, Donald V. "James Buchanan," in *Great Lives from History.* Edited by Frank N. Magill. Vol. 1. Pasadena, CA: Salem Press, 1987.

Weisbrot, Robert. *Freedom Bound: A History of America's Civil Rights Movement.* New York: W. W. Norton, 1990.

White, Richard, and Kevin Collins. *The United States Department of Homeland Security: An Overview.* New York: Pearson, 2005.

Widick, B. J. *Detroit: City of Race and Class Violence.* Chicago: Quadrangle, 1972.

Wilentz, Sean. *Andrew Jackson.* Edited by Arthur M. Schlesinger Jr. New York: Times Books / Henry Holt, 2005.

Williams, Juan, and Julian Bond. *Eyes on the Prize: America's Civil Rights Years, 1954–1965.* New York: Penguin, 1988.

Wills, Garry. *James Madison.* New York: Times Books, 2002.

Winders, Richard Bruce. *Mr. Polk's Army: The American Military Experience in the Mexican War.* College Station: Texas A&M University Press, 1997.

Wood, Trish, and Bobby Muller. *What Was Asked of Us: An Oral History of the Iraq War by the Soldiers Who Fought It.* Boston: Little, Brown, 2006.

Wormser, Richard. *The Rise and Fall of Jim Crow.* New York: St. Martin's Griffin, 2004.

Wright, Lawrence. *The Looming Tower: Al-Qaeda and the Road to 9/11.* New York: Knopf, 2006.

Zarefsky, David. *Lincoln, Douglas, and Slavery: In the Crucible of Public Debate.* Chicago: University of Chicago Press, 1990.

Zinn, Howard. *SNCC: The New Abolitionists.* Cambridge, MA: South End Press, 2002.

Periodicals

Balleck, Barry. "When the Ends Justify the Means: Thomas Jefferson and the Louisiana Purchase." *Presidential Quarterly* Vol. XVII, no. 4 (fall 1992).

Beck, Melinda, and Stryker McGuire. "Get Me Out of Here!," *Newsweek* (May 1, 1995).

Dotson, J. "An American Tragedy," *Newsweek* 70 (August 7, 1967): 18–26.

Drummond, Tammerlin. "Battling the Columbine Copycats." *Time* (May 10, 1999).

Grecco, Michael. "The Gurus of YouTube." *Time* (December 16, 2006).

Mandel, Michael J. "The Internet Economy." *Business Week* (February 22, 1999).

Shattuck, Kathryn. "Kerouac's 'Road' Scroll Is Going to Auction." *New York Times* (March 22, 2001).

"A Young Mayor Seeks an Answer in the Ashes," *Life* 63 (August 11, 1967): 21–22.

Web Sites

"Adoption Laws in the U.S." *The Task Force.* http://www.thetaskforce.org/downloads/reports/issue_maps/adoption_laws_09_07_color.pdf (accessed on July 21, 2008).

Africans in America. http://www.pbs.org/wgbh/aia/home.html (accessed on July 21, 2008).

The Air Force Association. http://www.afa.org/ (accessed on July 21, 2008).

Almasy, Steve. "The Internet Transforms Modern Life." *CNN.com*. http://www.cnn.com/2005/TECH/internet/06/23/evolution.main/index.html (accessed on July 21, 2008).

"Amelia Earhart's Last Flight." *Virtual Exploration Society*. http://www.unmuseum.org/earhart.htm (accessed on July 21, 2008).

"American Masters: Aaron Copland." *PBS.org*. http://www.pbs.org/wnet/americanmasters/database/copland_a.html (accessed on July 21, 2008).

"American Masters: McCarthyism." *PBS.org*. http://www.pbs.org/wnet/americanmasters/database/mccarthyism.html (accessed on July 21, 2008).

"American Visionaries: Tuskegee Airmen." *National Park Service*. http://www.nps.gov/museum/exhibits/tuskegee/airoverview.htm (accessed on July 21, 2008).

"Amistad Trials, 1839–40." *Famous American Trials*. http://www.law.umkc.edu/faculty/projects/ftrials/amistad/AMISTD.HTM (accessed on July 21, 2008).

"Andrew Carnegie." *PBS: American Experience*. http://www.pbs.org/wgbh/amex/carnegie/sfeature/meet.html (accessed on July 21, 2008).

Army.mil: The Official Homepage of the United States Army. http://www.army.mil/ (accessed on July 21, 2008).

"The Atlantic Slave Trade." *PBS: The Story of Africa: Slavery*. http://www.bbc.co.uk/worldservice/africa/features/storyofafrica/9chapter4.shtml (accessed on July 21, 2008).

Aviation-History.com. http://www.aviation-history.com/ (accessed on July 21, 2008).

BarackObama.com. http://www.barackobama.com/index.php (accessed on July 21, 2008).

"Bill Clinton (1946–)." *Miller Center of Public Affairs, University of Virginia*. http://www.millercenter.virginia.edu/academic/americanpresident/clinton (accessed on July 21, 2008).

Brain, Marshall. "How Biological and Chemical Warfare Works." *How Stuff Works*. http://science.howstuffworks.com/biochem-war4.htm (accessed on July 21, 2008).

"A Brief History." *Levittown Historical Society*. http://www.levittownhistoricalsociety.org/index2.htm (accessed on July 21, 2008).

"A Brief History of the American Red Cross." *RedCross.org*. http://www.redcross.org/museum/history/brief.asp (accessed on July 21, 2008).

"Brown v. Board of Education, 347 U.S. 483 (1954)." *The National Center for Public Policy Research*. http://www.nationalcenter.org/brown.html (accessed on July 21, 2008).

"The Call of the Wild." *SparkNotes.com*. http://www.sparknotes.com/lit/call/ (accessed on July 21, 2008).

"The Carter Family." *Southern Music Network.* http://www.southernmusic.net/carterfamily.htm (accessed on July 21, 2008).

Carter, Jimmy, and Amy Goodman. "Palestine: Peace Not Apartheid … Jimmy Carter in His Own Words." *Democracy Now!: The War and Peace Report.* http://www.democracynow.org/article.pl?sid=06/11/30/1452225 (accessed on July 21, 2008).

"Chasing the Sun: Aviation Timeline." *PBS.org.* http://www.pbs.org/kcet/chasingthesun/timeline/1900.html (accessed on July 21, 2008).

"Chief Joseph." *PBS: New Perspectives on the West.* http://www.pbs.org/weta/thewest/people/a_c/chiefjoseph.htm (accessed on July 21, 2008).

"Climate Change: Basic Information." *U.S. Environmental Protection Agency.* http://www.epa.gov/climatechange/basicinfo.html (accessed on July 22, 2008).

"Conflict of Abolition and Slavery." *The African American Mosaic: A Library of Congress Resource Guide for the Study of Black History and Culture.* http://www.loc.gov/exhibits/african/afam007.html (accessed on July 21, 2008).

"The Declaration of Sentiments, Seneca Falls Conference, 1848." *Modern History Sourcebook.* http://www.fordham.edu/halsall/mod/Senecafalls.html (acccessed on July 21, 2008).

"Despite Huge Katrina Relief, Red Cross Criticized." *MSNBC.com.* http://www.msnbc.msn.com/id/9518677/ (accessed on July 21, 2008).

"Directory of U.S. Political Parties." *Politics1.com.* http://politics1.com/parties.htm (accessed on July 21, 2008).

"Disco." *Streetswing.com.* http://www.streetswing.com/histmain/z3disco1.htm (accessed on July 21, 2008).

Discovery: Space. http://dsc.discovery.com/space/index.html (accessed on July 21, 2008).

"Domestic Security: The Homefront and the War on Terrorism. The USA PATRIOT Act." *PBS: The Online NewsHour.* http://www.pbs.org/newshour/indepth_coverage/terrorism/homeland/patriotact.html (accessed on July 21, 2008).

"The Doughboys of World War I." *OldMagazineArticles.com.* http://www.oldmagazinearticles.com/doughboys.php (accessed on July 21, 2008).

"Douglas MacArthur." *PBS: American Experience.* http://www.pbs.org/wgbh/amex/macarthur/ (accessed on July 21, 2008).

Drye, Willie. "America's Lost Colony: Can New Dig Solve Mystery?" *National Geographic.* http://news.nationalgeographic.com/news/2004/03/0302_040302_lostcolony.html (accessed on July 22, 2008).

Edithwharton.org. http://www.edithwharton.org/edithwharton/ (accessed on July 21, 2008).

Elvis Presley: The Official Site of the King of Rock 'n' Roll. http://www.elvis.com/ (accessed on July 21, 2008).

Erbsen, Wayne. "Origins of Bluegrass in Western North Carolina." *Native Ground Music.* http://www.nativeground.com/originsofbluegrass.asp (accessed on July 21, 2008).

"Executive Order 11246: Equal Employment Opportunity." *PBS: American Experience: The Presidents.* http://www.pbs.org/wgbh/amex/presidents/36_l_johnson/psources/ps_execorder.html (accessed on July 21, 2008).

"Facts for Features: Oldest Baby Boomers Turn 60!" *U.S. Census Bureau.* http://www.census.gov/Press-Release/www/releases/archives/facts_for_features_special_editions/006105.html (accessed on July 21, 2008).

"Fahrenheit 451." *SparkNotes.com.* http://www.sparknotes.com/lit/451/context.html (accessed on July 21, 2008).

Federal Communications Commission. http://www.fcc.gov/ (accessed on July 21, 2008).

"Fifteen Years of the Web." *BBC News.* http://news.bbc.co.uk/1/hi/technology/5243862.stm (accessed on July 21, 2008).

"First Baby Boomer Files for Social Security Benefits." *FoxNews.com.* http://www.foxnews.com/story/0,2933,301997,00.html (accessed on July 21, 2008).

"Fog of War: The Gulf War." *Washington Post.* http://www.washingtonpost.com/wp-srv/inatl/longterm/fogofwar/fogofwar.htm (accessed on July 21, 2008).

"Fort Raleigh: National Historical Site." *National Park Service.* http://www.cr.nps.gov/history/online_books/hh/16/hh16toc.htm (accessed on July 21, 2008).

Giangreco, D. M. and Robert E. Griffin. "Marshall Plan." *TrumanLibrary.org.* http://www.trumanlibrary.org/whistlestop/BERLIN_A/MARSHALL.HTM (accessed on July 21, 2008).

"Global HIV Prevalence Has Leveled Off; AIDS Is among the Leading Causes of Death Globally and Remains the Primary Cause of Death in Africa." *UNAIDS.org.* http://data.unaids.org/pub/EPISlides/2007/071119_epi_pressrelease_en.pdf (accessed on July 21, 2008).

"Grand Ole Opry." *Southern Music Network.* http://www.southernmusic.net/grandoleopry.htm (accessed on July 21, 2008).

"The Grapes of Wrath." *SparkNotes.com.* http://www.sparknotes.com/lit/grapesofwrath/ (accessed on July 21, 2008).

"The Great War and the Shaping of the 20th Century (World War I)." *PBS.org.* http://www.pbs.org/greatwar/ (accessed on July 21, 2008).

Gross, Terry. "Get on the Bus: The Freedom Riders of 1961." *NPR.org.* http://www.npr.org/templates/story/story.php?storyId=5149667 (accessed on July 21, 2008).

"The Gulf War." *PBS: Frontline.* http://www.pbs.org/wgbh/pages/frontline/gulf/ (accessed on July 21, 2008).

"Hate Crime Legislative Update." *National Association of Social Workers.* http://www.socialworkblog.org/advocacy/index.php/2008/01/11/hate-crime-legislative-update/ (accessed on July 21, 2008).

"Henry Kissinger." *Nobelprize.org.* http://nobelprize.org/nobel_prizes/peace/laureates/1973/kissinger-bio.html (accessed on July 21, 2008).

"Hillary Clinton." *WiseTo.* http://socialissues.wiseto.com/Election2008/HillaryClinton/ (accessed on July 21, 2008).

Hillouse, R. J. "Who Runs the CIA? Outsiders for Hire." *Washington Post.* http://www.washingtonpost.com/wp-dyn/content/article/2007/07/06/AR2007070601993_pf.html (accessed on July 21, 2008).

"Historic Construction Company Project—Transcontinental Railroad." *ConstructionCompany.com.* http://www.constructioncompany.com/historic-construction-projects/transcontinental-railroad/ (accessed on July 21, 2008).

"A Historical Overview." *U.S. Coast Guard.* http://www.uscg.mil/history/articles/h_USCGhistory.asp (accessed on July 21, 2008).

"History of the American Flag." *AmericanRevolution.com.* http://www.americanrevolution.com/HistoryoftheAmericanFlag.htm (accessed on July 21, 2008).

"The History of AT&T." *AT&T.com.* http://www.corp.att.com/history/ (accessed on July 21, 2008).

"History of the Court." *The Supreme Court Historical Society.* http://www.supremecourthistory.org/02_history/subs_history/02_c.html (accessed on July 21, 2008).

"History of the FBI." *Federal Bureau of Investigation.* http://www.fbi.gov/libref/historic/history/text.htm (accessed on July 21, 2008).

"A History of Gay and Lesbian Rights." *Public Agenda for Citizens.* http://www.publicagenda.org/citizen/issueguides/gay-rights (accessed on July 21, 2008).

"HIV and AIDS." *KidsHealth.com.* http://www.kidshealth.org/parent/infections/std/hiv.html (accessed on July 21, 2008).

"Invisible Man." *SparkNotes.com.* http://www.sparknotes.com/lit/invisibleman/ (accessed on July 21, 2008).

"Iraq Coalition Casualty Count." *Icasualties.org.* http://icasualties.org/oif/Details.aspx (accessed on July 21, 2008).

"Iraq Poll 2007." *BBC News.* http://news.bbc.co.uk/2/shared/bsp/hi/pdfs/19_03_07_iraqpollnew.pdf (accessed on July 21, 2008).

"Irving Berlin: The Dean of American Songwriters." *Parlorsongs.com.* http://parlorsongs.com/bios/berlin/iberlin.php (accessed on July 21, 2008).

"Jacqueline Lee Bouvier Kennedy." *The White House.* http://www.whitehouse .gov/history/firstladies/jk35.html (accessed on July 21, 2008).

"Jimmy Carter." *The White House.* http://www.whitehouse.gov/history/ presidents/jc39.html (accessed on July 21, 2008).

"John Brown's Raid on Harpers Ferry." *Secession Era Editorials Project.* http://history.furman.edu/benson/docs/jbmenu.htm (accessed on July 22, 2008).

"John D. Rockefeller, 1839–1937." *The Rockefeller Archive Center.* http://archive.rockefeller.edu/bio/jdrsr.php (accessed on July 21, 2008).

"John McCain." *WiseTo.* http://socialissues.wiseto.com/Election2008/ JohnMcCain/ (accessed on July 21, 2008).

Johnson, Amy E. Boyle. "Ray Bradbury: Fahrenheit 451 Misinterpreted." *LAWeekly.com.* http://www.laweekly.com/news/news/ray-bradbury-fahrenheit-451-misinterpreted/16524/ (accessed on July 21, 2008).

"Karl Marx, 1818–1883." *The History Guide.* http://www.historyguide.org/ intellect/marx.html (accessed on July 21, 2008).

The King Center. http://www.thekingcenter.org/ (accessed on July 21, 2008).

"The Know Nothing and the *American Crusader.*" *The Historical Society of Pennsylvania.* http://www.hsp.org/default.aspx?id=446 (accessed on July 21, 2008).

"The Korean War." *The Harry S. Truman Library & Museum.* http://www .trumanlibrary.org/whistlestop/study_collections/korea/large/index.htm (accessed on July 21, 2008).

"The Liberty Bell." *U.S. History.* http://www.ushistory.org/libertybell/ (accessed on July 21, 2008).

"The Life of Henry Ford." *The Henry Ford.* http://www.thehenryford.org/ exhibits/hf/ (accessed on July 21, 2008).

Lincoln, Abraham. "'House Divided' Speech." *The History Place.* http://www.historyplace.com/lincoln/divided.htm (accessed on July 21, 2008).

"Lincoln Memorial." *National Park Service, National Register of Historic Places.* http://www.nps.gov/nr/travel/wash/dc71.htm (accessed on July 21, 2008).

"Lusitania." *PBS Online—Lost Liners.* http://www.pbs.org/lostliners/ lusitania.html (accessed on July 21, 2008).

"Lyndon B. Johnson." *The White House.* http://www.whitehouse.gov/history/ presidents/lj36.html (accessed on July 21, 2008).

"Making Mount Rushmore." *AmericanParkNetwork.com.* http://www.american parknetwork.com/parkinfo/content.asp?catid=92&contenttypeid=16 (accessed on July 21, 2008).

"Marine Corps History." *GlobalSecurity.org.* http://www.globalsecurity.org/ military/agency/usmc/history.htm (accessed on July 21, 2008).

"Marshall Plan." *Spartacus Schoolnet.* http://www.spartacus.schoolnet.co.uk/USAmarshallP.htm (accessed on July 21, 2008).

"The Marshall Plan (1947)." *America.gov.* http://www.america.gov/st/washfile-english/2005/April/200504291439291CJsamohT0.6520502.html (accessed on July 21, 2008).

Murphy, Gerald. "About the Iroquois Constitution." *Modern History Sourcebook.* http://www.fordham.edu/halsall/mod/iroquois.html (accessed on July 21, 2008).

"Narrow Use of Affirmative Action Preserved in College Admissions." *Law Center: CNN.com.* http://www.cnn.com/2003/LAW/06/23/scotus.affirmative.action/ (accessed on July 22, 2008).

NASA.com. http://www.nasa.gov/ (accessed on July 21, 2008).

Nichols, Bill. "8,000 Desert during Iraq War." *USA Today.* http://www.usatoday.com/news/washington/2006-03-07-deserters_x.htm (accessed on July 21, 2008).

"1986: Seven Dead in Space Shuttle Disaster." *BBC: On This Day.* http://news.bbc.co.uk/onthisday/hi/dates/stories/january/28/newsid_2506000/2506161.stm (accessed on July 21, 2008).

Oberg, James. "Seven Myths About the Challenger Shuttle Disaster." *MSNBC.com.* http://www.msnbc.msn.com/id/11031097/ (accessed on July 21, 2008).

"Oklahoma Bombing Report." *Washington Post.* http://www.washingtonpost.com/wp-srv/national/longterm/oklahoma/oklahoma.htm (accessed on July 21, 2008).

"Oklahoma City Tragedy." *CNN Interactive.* http://www.cnn.com/US/OKC/bombing.html (accessed on July 21, 2008).

"Paris Peace Talks." *PBS: American Experience.* http://www.pbs.org/wgbh/amex/honor/peopleevents/e_paris.html (accessed on July 21, 2008).

"The People's Vote: 100 Documents That Shaped America: The Truman Doctrine." *U.S. News & World Report.* http://www.usnews.com/usnews/documents/docpages/document_page81.htm (accessed on July 21, 2008).

"Peter, Paul and Mary." *Classicbands.com.* http://www.classicbands.com/ppm.html (accessed on July 21, 2008).

Peterson, Richard A. "Ten Things You Didn't Know about the Origins of Country Music." *University of Chicago Press.* http://www.press.uchicago.edu/Misc/Chicago/662845.html (accessed on July 21, 2008).

"Presidential Impeachment Proceedings: Bill Clinton, 42nd President." *The History Place.* http://www.historyplace.com/unitedstates/impeachments/clinton.htm (accessed on July 21, 2008).

"Sandra Day O'Connor." *National Women's Hall of Fame.* http://www .greatwomen.org/women.php?action=viewone&id=115 (accessed on July 21, 2008).

Scaruffi, Piero. "A Brief History of Country Music." *Scaruffi.com.* http://www.scaruffi.com/history/country.html (accessed on July 21, 2008).

Selective Service System. http://www.sss.gov/ (accessed on July 21, 2008).

SNCC 1960–66: Six Years of the Student Nonviolent Coordinating Committee. http://www.ibiblio.org/sncc/rides.html (accessed on July 22, 2008).

"Space Shuttle Columbia Disaster." *AerospaceGuide.net.* http://www .aerospaceguide.net/spaceshuttle/columbia_disaster.html (accessed on July 21, 2008).

"Teaching with Documents: The *Amistad* Case." *The National Archives.* http://www.archives.gov/education/lessons/amistad/ (accessed on July 22, 2008).

"They Changed the World: The Story of the Montgomery Bus Boycott, 1955–56." *Montgomery Advertiser.* http://www.montgomeryboycott .com/frontpage.htm (accessed on July 22, 2008).

"This Week in History: October." *Peacebuttons.info.* http://www .peacebuttons.info/E-News/peacehistoryoctober.htm (accessed on July 21, 2008).

"Thomas Jefferson Memorial." *National Park Service.* http://www.nps.gov/thje/ (accessed on July 21, 2008).

"Three Mile Island: The Inside Story." *Smithsonian National Museum of American History.* http://americanhistory.si.edu/tmi/ (accessed on July 21, 2008).

"Three Mile Island: The Judge's Ruling." *PBS Frontline: Nuclear Reaction.* http://www.pbs.org/wgbh/pages/frontline/shows/reaction/readings/tmi .html (accessed on July 21, 2008).

"The Time 100: Billy Graham." *Time.com.* http://www.time.com/time/ time100/heroes/profile/graham01.html (accessed on July 21, 2008).

"The Time 100: Louis B. Mayer." *Time.com.* http://www.time.com/time/ time100/builder/profile/mayer.html (accessed on July 21, 2008).

"The Time 100: Mao Zedong." *Time.com.* http://www.time.com/time/ time100/leaders/profile/mao.html (accessed on July 21, 2008).

"The Time 100: Martin Luther King." *Time.com.* http://www.time.com/time/ time100/leaders/profile/king.html (accessed on July 21, 2008).

"The Time 100: Rosa Parks." *Time.com.* http://www.time.com/time/ time100/heroes/profile/parks01.html (accessed on July 22, 2008).

"The Time 100: William Levitt." *Time.com.* http://www.time.com/time/ time100/builder/profile/levitt.html (accessed on July 21, 2008).

Trinklein, Mike, and Steve Boettcher. "The Oregon Trail." *Idaho State University.* http://www.isu.edu/%7Etrinmich/Oregontrail.html (accessed on July 22, 2008).

"Twenty-third Amendment." *JusticeLearning.org.* http://www.justicelearning .org/justice_timeline/Amendments.aspx?id=22 (accessed on July 21, 2008).

"The Underground Railroad." *National Geographic Online.* http://www.national geographic.com/railroad/ (accessed on July 22, 2008).

United States House of Representatives. http://www.house.gov/ (accessed on July 21, 2008).

"U.S. Constitutional Amendments." *FindLaw.com.* http://caselaw.lp.findlaw .com/data/constitution/amendments.html (accessed on July 21, 2008).

"U.S. Electoral College." *National Archives and Records Admininstration.* http://www.archives.gov/federal-register/electoral-college/faq.html#why electoralcollege (accessed on July 21, 2008).

"U.S.-Mexican War, 1846–1848." *PBS.org.* http://www.pbs.org/kera/ usmexicanwar/index_flash.html (accessed on July 22, 2008).

"U.S. Military Deaths in Iraq War at 4,124." *MSNBC.com.* http://www .msnbc.msn.com/id/5972698/ (accessed on July 21, 2008).

The U.S. Navy. http://www.navy.mil/swf/index.asp (accessed on July 21, 2008).

"Vietnam Online." *PBS.org.* http://www.pbs.org/wgbh/amex/vietnam/ (accessed on July 21, 2008).

The Vietnam Veterans Memorial. http://thewall-usa.com/information.asp (accessed on July 21, 2008).

Wagner, Steven. "How Did the Taft-Hartley Act Come About?" *History News Network.* http://hnn.us/articles/1036.html (accessed on July 21, 2008).

"The Washington Monument." *National Park Service.* http://www.nps.gov/ wamo/ (accessed on July 21, 2008).

"Weapons of Mass Destruction." *National Geographic.com.* http://magma .nationalgeographic.com/ngm/0211/feature1/ (accessed on July 22, 2008).

"Worldwide HIV & AIDS Statistics." *Avert.org.* http://www.avert.org/ worldstats.htm (accessed on July 21, 2008).

Index

Italic type indicates volume number; **boldface** indicates main entries' page numbers; (ill.) indicates photos and illustrations.

F

I

L

M

N

O

Sitka (Native American tribe), *6:* 1098

Sitting Bull, *6:* 1089, 1236–37; *7:* **1412–13;** *8:* 1727

Sixteenth Amendment, *7:* **1413–14;** *8:* 1508

Sixteenth Street Baptist Church, *1:* 159–60

Sixth Amendment, *7:* **1414–15**

60 Minutes (television program), *6:* 1148

Skaggs, Ricky, *2:* 401

Skyscrapers, *7:* **1415–17,** 1416 (ill.); *8:* 1616–17

Slater, Samuel, *4:* 765, 765 (ill.); *5:* 928

Slave rebellions, *7:* **1417–22,** 1419 (ill.), 1426, 1429

Slave ships and the Middle Passage, *1:* 110–11; *7:* **1422–26,** 1423 (ill.)

Slavery, *7:* **1426–31,** 1427. *See also* Abolition movement; Civil War

    Amistad insurrection, *1:* 72–75

    antebellum period, *7:* 1428–35

    Atlantic slave trade, *1:* 107–12; *2:* 462; *7:* 1422–26, 1423 (ill.), 1432; *8:* 1569

    Buchanan, James, on, *1:* 200

    Calhoun, John C., on, *2:* 223–24

    Clay, Henry, on, *2:* 318–19

    Columbus, Christopher, and, *2:* 363

    Compromise of 1850, *2:* 319, 370–71; *3:* 560, 612–13; *5:* 845; *6:* 1230–31; *8:* 1516, 1601

    cotton, *2:* 398–400, 399 (ill.); *4:* 767; *7:* 1429–30, 1431–32, 1434

    Democratic Party on, *3:* 584

    Dred Scott case, *2:* 463–66, 464 (ill.); *5:* 907, 1013; *7:* 1503–4

    Emancipation Proclamation, *1:* 134; *2:* 313; *3:* 496–99; *7:* 1431; *8:* 1553

    encomienda system, *3:* 504–6; *5:* 894; *6:* 1139–40

    end of, *1:* 9–10; *2:* 315–16; *5:* 910–11

    expansion, *2:* 310–11; *5:* 846, 913; *7:* 1285, 1310, 1372–73

    Fillmore, Millard, on, *3:* 560

    Freedmen's Bureau, *3:* 585; *7:* 1300, 1302

    Fugitive slave laws, *3:* 610–14, 611 (ill.); *7:* 1489; *8:* 1516, 1585, 1601

    Hispaniola, *5:* 893–94

    "House Divided" speech (Lincoln), *5:* 913

    Jefferson, Thomas, *4:* 823–24

    Kansas-Nebraska Act, *2:* 311; *5:* 843–47, 907, 913, 1012–13; *6:* 1231, 1248–49

    Lincoln, Abraham, *5:* 914–15; *8:* 1605

    Missouri Compromise, *2:* 310–11, 319, 370; *5:* 845, 907, 913, 928, 1010–13, 1011 (ill.), 1020, 1249; *6:* 1249, 1252

    Native North Americans of the Southeast, *6:* 1109

    Northwest Ordinance, *4:* 821

    Pierce, Franklin, *6:* 1231–32

    plantations, *7:* 1432–35, 1433 (ill.)

    Radical Republicans, *7:* 1285–86

    rebellions, *7:* 1417–22, 1426

    secession, *2:* 311, 372–73, 422–23; *3:* 497–98; *4:* 833; *5:* 908–9; *7:* 1299 (ill.), 1371–74, 1372 (ill.), 1489–90; *8:* 1516, 1604–5

    Seminole maroons, *7:* 1418–19

    slave codes, *7:* 1422, 1433–34

    state vs. federal government, *3:* 544

    Supreme Court, *7:* 1430

    Texas, *8:* 1540–41

    thirteen colonies, *1:* 109–10; *7:* 1426–28

    Thirteenth Amendment, *2:* 315; *5:* 911; *7:* 1303, 1431; *8:* 1553–55

    Transcendentalism, *8:* 1572

    Truth, Sojourner, *8:* 1581 (ill.), 1581–83

    Turner, Nat, *7:* 1419 (ill.), 1421–22

    Uncle Tom's Cabin (Stowe), *8:* 1601–2, 1604

    Underground Railroad, *2:* 460; *5:* 1033; *8:* 1583–85, 1602–4

    Webster, Daniel, *8:* 1678

    West Virginia, *8:* 1679

    Whig Party, *3:* 584; *8:* 1688

Slavery in the antebellum South, *7:* **1431–35**

Slidell, John, *5:* 995, 995 (ill.)

Slim Shady, *4:* 700–701

Smalls, Biggie, *4:* 699–700

Smith Act. *See* Alien Registration Act

Smith, Bessie, *4:* 675

Smith, Jedediah Strong, *3:* 616

Smith, John, *4:* 809; *6:* 1241–42; *7:* 1436 (ill.), **1436–40,** 1437 (ill.); *8:* 1547, 1637

Smith, Joseph, *2:* 281–83; *8:* 1742–43

Smith, Mamie, *4:* 676

Smith, Patti, *7:* 1331

W

X

Y

Z